Transforming the Workplace

John Nora
C. Raymond Rogers and
Robert Stramy

Princeton Research Press
Princeton, New Jersey

Transforming the Workplace

(The **integration** of Quality, Productivity and Quality of Worklife for the Global Challenge)

Published by Princeton Research Press
a division of Kepner-Tregoe, Inc.
P.O. Box 704
Princeton, N.J. 08540

Library of Congress Catalog Card No. 85-63213.

ISBN 0-936231-02-5

Manufactured in the United States of America

ACKNOWLEDGEMENTS

The authors wish to thank the men and women at the General Motors Livonia engine plant who made this book possible.

The authors also wish to thank the United Auto Workers and General Motors for their willingness to share the Livonia story through this book. By authorizing the publishing of this book, General Motors does not endorse or sponsor the process outlined in this book or the individual training used such as Kepner-Tregoe training processes.

The authors thank Mr. Ronald Herder of Manhattanville College for his excellent contribution in editing this book.

TRANSFORMING THE WORKPLACE

Table of Contents

FOREWORD

Surely the average Japanese auto worker is not 4,440 times more intelligent and energetic than the American worker? Well, at least one statistic would lead us to believe that's the case. The average Japanese worker at Toyota, Nissan or Honda, the authors report, submits 27 suggestions a year, 24 of which (90%) are accepted and implemented. On average, only one out of 37 American workers submits a suggestion, and only 20% of those are accepted (effectively meaning that only one out of 185 American workers has a suggestion accepted). Multiply the 24 by the 185 and you get a factor of 4,440! You might quibble with the exact numbers, but you can't quibble with the point they project. There's a problem! Or, as John Nora, Raymond Rogers and Robert Stramy put it, "The simple truth of the 1980's is: we are in deadly serious trouble." They go on, "There must be a top to bottom industrial transformation. There are few other options worth talking about."

The Nora/Rogers/Stramy conclusion is not a novel one. Unfortunately, however, most other books go on to talk about solutions in terms of needed federal policy to "make the playing field level" and various machinations of tax reform to enhance investment in smokestack industries. While I am in agreement that government policy toward investment and foreign competition is vital, ignored in the fray is the people aspect. And the story of *Transforming the Workplace*, thank heavens, is pure and simple a people story. It's the key actors' story of the 1979 through 1984 transformation of the Livonia Cadillac engine works of the General Motors Corporation, under the vital leadership of Bob Stramy, then plant manager (he has since moved on to head a major GM activity in Mexico).

In 1979 Livonia employed 400 people; today, after major retooling and a thoroughgoing restructuring of the work environment, it employs 1400—and that number continues to climb. Productivity has

v

been increased well over 100%, and cost has been reduced 50%. At least as significant, quality is at the very top of the heap, customer complaints are down radically, and warranty claims have been reduced to virtually none. Machine up time has risen over a third, absenteeism is down more than 50%. It's a whopping success story, from the heart of the rust bowl to boot.

But it's more than a success story. The book's title uses the appropriate word: transformation. It talks about just what **can** be done. The authors quote Bill Abernathy (who tragically passed away in 1984) and Kim Clark, in *The Industrial Renaissance*: "Imagine an American plant (Livonia) with no executive parking or dining areas, no general foreman, relatively few support staff, no multi-classification systems for job descriptions and compensation, workers (all union members) divided into teams with responsibility for production, quality control, materials handling, and the like. Further, imagine the whole had been planned by a committee on which sat four union members as active participants. A figment of the imagination? Not at all." The Livonia story **is** unimaginable in the American context of the early 1970's, when complacency still reigned. Today, sadly, it is still far from commonplace. Nonetheless, it is a bellwether, a herald of what could be.

Fortunately, as exciting as the Livonia story is, *Transforming the Workplace* is not merely a case study. The authors' goal is no less than to provide a guide for transformation of American industry. Thus the Livonia story is used as the meat, but the book, above all, offers a very practical outline for people who would try to replicate the process. The detail is extraordinary; for instance, when describing how to put together a first orientation workshop for management and union leadership, the authors go so far as to recommend specific books to read from which to take communications exercises that could be used on the first night.

Such mundane detail, which may win the book little applause from sociologist or business school professor critic, is exactly what's missing in most other books of the genre (including both of my own!).

Two thrusts work simultaneously: the process by which the Livonia project got up and running is analyzed (perhaps 70% of the material), and the specifics are covered (the other 30%) such as details of the analysis that led Livonia to decide to take the bold step of getting rid of the General Foreman and Foreman job categories.

Over and over, the authors reiterate that "the process of implementation is more important than the specific changes implemented," despite the impressive nature of the specific changes. Their process description, for those who might be fearful, is not some kind of a rehash of the organization development books of the 1960's (though the authors pay appropriate tribute to, especially, Rensis Likert, whose foresight from the 1940's is finally, belatedly, being realized today).

The "organizational development" aspects of the book are, above all, pragmatic. For instance, the first meeting of the union and management is outlined in great detail, including an outline sketch of the opening remarks that were made.

Following the initial agreement to proceed, the Livonia project (subsequently and appropriately named the "Livonia Opportunity") moved into the selection and development of the Livonia Planning Team. I found this to be the most exciting part of the book. Most certainly agree that a planning team is necessary; in the Livonia process it was critical. The 15 member team required half of the members' time for a full year! The team's selection, training and activities are spelled out in vivid detail.

Vast amounts of team time were spent on some pretty sophisticated sociological and anthropological analysis (described in a jargon free fashion)—learning about the different interlocking natures of quality systems, training, collective bargaining agreements, organizational structures, compensation planning, workflow design, communications, physical environment, overall operating philosophy of the organization, formal organizations, informal organizations, power structures, relationships,... and on. There was no effort to soft-pedal the task. Again and again the authors remind that it's essential to take a complex, detailed, analysis-driven look at **all** the factors which underpin the enhancement of "quality, productivity and quality of work life." They are appropriately critical of band aid programs that they describe as "piecemeal, public relations window dressing, and (those that focus on) the appealing glamor of short term change." The task they set out is a formidable one. Fortunately, the tools to do the job are laid out in enough detail to be of very specific value to anyone who has the guts to mount such a program.

Once you have struggled with your colleagues through the trials and tribulations of the planning team activities, you might think you've got it knocked. They quickly disabuse us of that notion when they move into the next staggering aspect—implementation in the organization itself. A specific part of their message is one that I invariably find missing in most implementation analyses. They comment that "change is a fragile, vulnerable thing," and then talk at length about the issue of timing. In particular, they recommend not moving too fast. Ducks must be lined up. Decades of skepticism must be stripped away. It doesn't happen overnight, or even in the first 18 months. (In my book, *A Passion for Excellence*, with Nancy Austin, one of our most detailed studies describes the transformation of textile superstar Milliken & Company, in an equally battered industry. Our findings parallel those of the Livonia team: timing is practically everything, and "slow down and give it a chance to take hold" is the central message.)

The process is the key, but the specifics are exciting, too. The Livonia Planning Team began by debating for months to arrive at a formal organizational philosophy—the Livonia Engine Plant Operating Philosophy, which is reproduced in the book. Following upon the heels of the philosophy and much analysis of how things had gotten to be the way they were came the principal finding: "The most powerful and influential conclusion concerns the Livonia Planning Team's unqualified support and promotion of the team concept as a central and unifying force throughout the new organization. So urgent and prominent was this ideal, moreover, that it immediately became the recurrent main theme of the evolving operating plan and its orchestration over the months of planned implementation." A team focus meant that every person in the organization became reorganized into eight to fifteen person groups. Importantly, the group's designation changed from Work Group to Business Team. The Business Team is a highly autonomous group (especially by prior standards) responsible for scheduling, training and problem solving.

From the team focus, many other conclusions followed. Most astonishing to me was the decision to get rid of the General Foreman layer of management entirely. The next level, the Foreman level, was supplanted in title by a vital new designation: Team Coordinator (and in the final organization there were almost 40% fewer Team Coordinators than there would have been Foremen following traditional span of control logic).

Union-management cooperation was vital at every step along the way, from the first glimmer of an idea through every stage of implementation. Hourly union members sat prominently on the Planning Team (30% representation), which had a charter that allowed it to intrude into any aspect of organization, no matter how sacred—meaning, in particular, access to previously top secret information.

Thus, management eliminated unnecessary layers, constraints and supervision (quality control, for instance, was moved into production operations over time), and the union responded with like simplifying measures. In particular, all job distinctions were done away with, and the typical manufacturing, quality control, material handling designations were reduced to but one: Quality Operator. Moreover, the Quality Operators proceeded through a "pay-for-knowledge" program, by which they were encouraged to learn virtually every job in the plant.

Concerning union-management relations, the dreamed-for "Team Coordinator **and** (union) rep engaged in joint problem solving" was achieved rather than the traditional "foremen **versus** union rep."

In addition to these heart of the matter accomplishments, many other heretofore unheard of activities became part and parcel of the implementation process: elimination of private parking spots and supervisorial dining rooms; shirt sleeves and no tie replacing white shirts and ties on the part of management; team suggestion awards and individual suggestion awards (with a primary focus on the team); widespread information sharing, based upon 40 hard nosed performance indicators (performance indicators that were designed **by the teams**); regular team (weekly) and all hands plant meetings; a weekly plant newspaper; employee involvement in plant decorations; appraisal programs focused upon the individual's support of the business team; transfers and job rotations as an anytime proposition, with no muss and fuss; development of technical support teams in a role of **assisting** (not dictating to) the Business Teams.

I've had the privilege of knowing Bob Stramy for a couple of years. Since Bob is one of the authors, the role of committed, caring leadership is touched upon, but is not an overpowering part of the book's message. Stramy is too humble. My experience with him, with a counterpart, Phil Staley, who transformed a Ford assembly plant in Edison, New Jersey and a handful of others of their ilk suggests their role is more monumental than is proposed between these covers. The book at times (despite its successful effort to focus on the details of process) is a bit too positive in this sense: many of the minor triumphs described required exceptional personal commitment, patience, and a willingness to turn the other cheek in the face of abuse by all the major power players involved (company management, union management, foremen, general foremen, rank and file membership, staff specialists and so on).

The book in no way presents a cut and dried formula. It provides many careful guidelines and suggestions, but these will have to be substantially tailored to any particular circumstance. It sets out, in more detail than I've ever seen before, the specifics and the process of a genuine transformation. Moreover, it holds out as carrot the awesome potential that can be released if such a process, with local adaption, is patiently pursued by others.

Along the way the authors quote Robert Reich's "The Next American Frontier," "America's place in the evolving world economy will increasingly depend on its worker's skills, vigor, initiative, and capacity for collaboration and adaptation. Our future lies in our human capital.'' I'm sorry to say that even today, in reading the formal public statements of the heads of auto companies, steel companies and those in the most battered segments of the economy, the people side of the industrial equation still merits short shrift next to the exotica of automation and the preoccupation with ''the S.O.B.'s in Washington.'' Our necessary industrial transformation will require retooling and new policy, but most of all it will require a totally new view of what people can do if the adversarial management-work force relations are removed and if both sides address what can be done cooperatively. The Livonia Opportunity provides a bright beacon: ''Initial concern, anxiety, even fear is replaced in time by a sense of self-fulfillment, achievement, advancement and—that rarest of plant visitors—pleasure in one's craft.'' Bravo!

Tom Peters

(Mr. Peters is co-author of *In Search of Excellence* and *A Passion for Excellence*.)

PART ONE

Chapter 1

The **Integration** of Quality, Productivity and Quality of Worklife for the Global Challenge

American Industry is fast losing the global industrial race. Our trade **deficit** in manufactured goods has grown significantly in recent years. Where American industry once led the world in productivity it is now playing a panicky game of catch-up ball.

We once listened to our RCA radio and watched our Zenith television, plugged in our G.E. clock, clicked our Kodak camera and drove the latest car out of Detroit. Today our homes are warehouses of Sonys, Sanyos, Seikos, Panasonics, Nikons or Canons; and our roads, the parade grounds for a vast fleet of Japanese and German imports. Our calculators, computers and electronic typewriters are imports. Our watches, TVs and sewing machines are imports. We play a Yamaha piano, ride a Honda motorcycle and compete with imported sports equipment. We build with Kobe steel and farm with Mitsubishi tractors.

1

For every one of these products accepted by the domestic and international consumer, an American-made product goes unsold, the job security of an American worker is threatened, and our collective standard of living deteriorates.

American industrial strength was once the envy of all nations. Life was secure. Jobs were secure. The future was a safe harbor for our children. From 1960 to the present America's key industries have been hit hard. In our domestic market we are talking about serious declines in steel, rubber, apparel, electrical components, farm machinery, food processing machinery, textile machinery, industrial inorganic chemicals, consumer electronics, footwear, metal-cutting and metal-forming machine tools and calculating machines. In 1985, elimination of voluntary import restrictions seriously threatened the automobile assembly and parts supply industries after a temporary upswing.

In world markets we are talking about serious declines in motor vehicles, aircraft, organic chemicals, telecommunications apparatus, plastic materials, nonelectronic machinery and appliances, medical and pharmaceutical products, metal-working machinery, agricultural machinery, hand and machine tools, textile and leather machinery, railway vehicles and housing fixtures.

Jobs are in jeopardy as industries in the industrial North are shut down and production is transferred to areas or countries where labor costs are comparatively low. As developing countries such as Korea, Taiwan, Brazil and Mexico convert to high-volume, standardized production, American competitiveness is lost.

Lulled by the periodic or seasonal upswing in this industry or that, there are those among us who will still refuse to confront the simple truth of the 1980s: we are in deadly serious trouble. We face a choice of obsolescence or transformation. We had better begin listening and do something about it, as Owen Bieber, President of the United Auto Workers, notes:

> The economy sails along until we go over a waterfall. Then everybody bails like hell to try to surface the boat; some people drown. Once again we get over that mess and go floating along again, nobody gives a hoot . . . How many times can you go over? How many people can drown before the boat is empty?[1]

Did we reach the cliff's edge all by ourselves? Or did the world push us? Our inability to compete in the world-wide market has been blamed on (among other factors):

- the value of the dollar
- detrimental government regulations
- prohibitive union demands and adversarial relationships with management
- outdated plants and equipment
- commitment to high-volume, standardized production
- cutbacks in research and development
- cultural differences between the United States and other nations, especially Japan
- unfair marketing practices by world competitors

There has not been, nor does there continue to be, much agreement over causes among our leading economists and business analysts.

Be that as it may, America's industrial leaders have been appallingly shortsighted—if a 30-year-old blindness may be so called. Present day authors and management consultants comment on this blindness as follows: Warren Bennis says American companies concentrate on doing things right instead of **doing the right things**. George Ainsworth-Land says that leaders have been replaced by managers with a short-term mentality, trying to repeat today what was successful yesterday. Robert Reich laments American industry's inability to shift from high-volume, standardized production to flexible, skill-intensive production. He reports that America's business leaders have tried to maintain short-term profits through legal and financial maneuvers he calls "paper entrepreneurialism."[2]

Now, forced into an awareness that previously eluded them, American industrial leaders **appear** prepared to grasp a few simple truths:

- Markets have become global, and **we are not competitive**.

- In the semi-skilled, high-volume, standardized production, typical of developing countries who work to capacity with cheap labor, **we are not competitive**.

- In the flexible skill-intensive production typical of European and Japanese companies, **we are not competitive**.

Tough problems demand tough responses. To the charges of their noncompetitive stance American producers can answer defensively, and continue without significant change, or respond in a way appropriate to their survival. **The survival response is obviously to take steps toward providing a high-quality product at a competitive price to a world market.**

If this worthwhile goal demands that old habits be broken, new systems and structures be developed, and new relationships be nurtured, so be it. If low-skilled work will continue to flow to developing countries and our niche in the global market is to be high-technology, precision production, let the process of training, growth and development begin. If survival of American business must in fact be equated with top-to-bottom industrial transformation, then there are few other options worth talking about.

Japan is a good teacher.

Before 1960, the sticker "Made in Japan" was synonymous with shoddy goods and glue-and-staple manufacturing. Faced with a survival crisis, several Japanese industries quietly made the transformation to excellence while we complacently appreciated the value of good old American craftsmanship. We valued our pride.

By the late 1970s our industrial leaders needed an effective jolt. Japan supplied it swiftly by positive example, 70% of employees at all levels in the organization are involved in problem solving and decision making. In American auto companies only 12% of employees— **all in higher level positions**—are involved in these same basic processes.

In the plants of Toyota, Honda and Nissan, employees submit an average of 27 suggestions per person, per year. At Toyota alone, over 90% of suggestions made are adopted, 3,365 suggestions are implemented per day, savings are over 30 million dollars! Contrast this degree of involvement, participation and communication with the American yearly average of one suggestion per 37 auto employees, with an implementation rate of just over 20%.

Why the difference? While American industry focuses primarily on investment in capital equipment, the Japanese auto companies invest simultaneously in capital equipment, state of the art technology and human resources. Japanese auto workers receive five times more training per year than their American counterparts, resulting in a well-trained, committed workforce, consistently involved in decision making and problem solving, and directly responsible for quality and productivity.

The American worker, on the other hand, has become the victim of an industrial system that neither acknowledges, values, nor profits by his or her potential to contribute to the corporation. As industry moved from unit production to mass production and then to continuous-process production, line supervisors lost control to new layer upon layer of management. This structural change shifted responsibility for quality and productivity from worker to supervisor to manager, with a predictable (but ignored) chain reaction: worker alienation . . . job disinterest . . . deteriorating quality . . . a down slide in productivity.

> There is no way that a rigid, hierarchical, standardized production system can compete for long with a flexible system that enjoys the cooperative support of all its people . . . For the United States, however, the shift has been slow and painful . . . the transition requires a basic restructuring of business, labor and government.[3]

Recently, after a thirty-year sleep, American industrialists woke up to the issue of global competitiveness—**yet without fully addressing the far more fundamental issue of human resource development**—many of them implementing various forms of programs to improve quality, productivity or quality of worklife.

There is a powerful temptation to applaud these canned program advances—for who in good faith would not delight in **any** change for the better? But despite some positive results, we must look past piecemeal programs, occasional public-relations window dressing, and especially the appealing glamour of short-term change.

Despite all these things we must remain clear-eyed and aware of a single fundamental issue: **In its effort toward organizational transformation, American industry has no powerful central operating philosophy**.

If the answer is not in piecemeal change, it must lie elsewhere.

While consultants are making profits, business is not closing the competitive gap. Deming and Juran insist we install Statistical Quality Control. *Business Week* calls for a complete "reindustrialization of America."[4] Authors advise us to learn from Japanese management methods. Businesses are rushing to install employee participation groups and new socio-technical systems. Employees from numerous industries are attending quality awareness sessions. We are awash in a sea of diverse advice.

Is it any wonder that the operating manager is confused, having to decide whom to believe, what to believe, and what to do about it?

The search for answers is no less complex than the search for causes of our decline. It seems clear, however, that hasty remedies, rapidly applied, with a goal of short-term results, will not work. Short-term thinking is no answer. Our typical "Band-Aid" business philosophy is no solution. Technological advances alone are not enough. Head count reductions are not enough. Standardized quality and inventory control programs are not enough. Piecemeal "quality of worklife" programs or training programs are not enough.

What will be enough is workplace transformation: comprehensive and integrated change in business philosophy, expectations, responsibilities, structure, employee development, compensation systems, communications, teamwork, trust, the working environment, operating systems, work rules and all industrial relationships.

If transformation is the only viable, workable, lasting solution, then we must immediately concern ourselves with solving the most glaring fault of our traditional system: **American industry has all but ignored the opportunity to improve quality, increase productivity, and develop flexibility through radically improved utilization of human resources.**

> Without human strengths, new machinery, advanced techniques and elaborate strategies are not worth a farthing. If the reservoir is allowed to run dry, no sudden burst of management attention can set things to rights. Bare survival may be possible at least for a while, but response to change (the hallmark of industrial vitality) is not[5].

To our detriment American industry is to this day characterized by **adversarial** relations between union and management, between worker and supervisor, and within the management ranks, and by a salaried and hourly workforce whose goals and loyalties are *not* consistent with those of the organization.

Does any of this sound familiar?

The Voice of Management:

"Give 'em an inch and they'll take a mile" . . . "They don't care about quality or production; they've lost the work ethic" . . . "They have no pride of workmanship" . . . "Eight hours pay for eight hours work" . . . "I don't care, five more years and I can retire" . . .

The Voice of the Worker:

"Management can't be trusted" . . . "They don't give a damn about quality—only profit and production" . . . "I'm paid to do my job; management is paid to think" . . . "Do any more and it'll be expected all the time" . . . "They treat you like a child, what do they expect?" . . .

The Voice of the Union:

"How can we cooperate with management on operating issues? We can't even agree on the location of a water fountain!" . . . "We're political; we can't look like we're cooperating" . . . "Our only responsibility is to protect our people from those crazy foremen . . ."

It doesn't have to be this way:

What we create, we can transform.

At Livonia we developed a process of transformation comprehensive and innovative enough to generate improvements in quality, productivity and quality of worklife, to develop the structure, systems and relationships truly appropriate to a highly skilled workforce, and to attract the first-hand attention of international managers and of the American business press.

> In the 1980s . . . the Japanese have changed in a fundamental way the terms on which competition in the automobile industry must be carried out. The imperatives of quality and productivity, which lie at the heart of this new industrial competition, are impossible to satisfy without the active, loyal and committed participation of a well-trained and constantly improving workforce. . . .

> Imagine an American plant with no executive parking or dining areas, no general foreman, relatively few support staff, no multiclassification systems for job descriptions and compensation, workers (all union members) divided into teams with responsibility for production, quality control, materials handling, and the like. Further, imagine the whole had been planned by a committee on which sat four union members as active participants. A figment of the imagination? Not at all. It is the Cadillac Engine Plant in Livonia, Michigan, which along with many other facilities is rapidly demonstrating that a new American paradigm for production is indeed possible at the level of workforce management.[6]

PART TWO

INTRODUCTION

What you have just read is history. What you are about to read is a story about people who are proving that a comprehensive change for the better is a workable, practical alternative to a traditional system that no longer works. It is a story that has brightened the lives of its authors, the people we work with every day, the fortunes of an organization, and our attitude toward the possibilities of worklife in America.

The story is about what we started in 1979 at an engine plant in Livonia, Michigan, and about a process of transformation that is going on even as you read these words. This transformation is real, visible and verifiable. It has generated the results we had hoped for: significant improvement in product quality, productivity and quality of worklife to regain domestic dominance, while at the same time development of the systems, structures, skills and relationships necessary to compete world-wide in high-technology, precision and skilled production. The transformation demanded by global competition and the need to continually improve the standard of living in America was made.

If, however, Livonia's story had no wider application, it would forever remain an anomaly, and little more than an interesting footnote in some future History of American Industry. That this is hardly the case has been confirmed by others who have adopted our approach to transform their workplace. This validates the worth and appropriateness of our work and reaffirms what we believed in from the start:

8

. . . that it is possible to transform any organization to meet the competitive challenge;

. . . that transformation is an attractive, practical, workable alternative to traditional ways of doing business;

. . . that the essential ingredients present at Livonia either already exist in other industries, corporations, and business enterprises or can be generated to begin a transformation process—regardless of size or the nature of their current products or services.

Livonia's story should therefore be read as an *application* of this transformation process, with the understanding that each step we took and every stage we passed through are, with appropriate variations, fully transferrable to other organizations, new or old. It is not the specific changes made at Livonia that are important, it is the process by which the changes were planned and implemented that holds the key to the future.

In fact, following work at Livonia the transformation process has been improved and used both inside and outside the auto industry. The Livonia experiment is an ambitious, exciting effort at total, comprehensive workforce transformation. Since its inception in 1979, improvements in the approach have continued to be made. And with refinements, the basic approach will continue to contribute to the health and well being of the organization.

The "Review **Guidelines** Application" sections introduced at the end of Chapter 2 are intended as digests for the reader who finds value in both our process and the possibilities of its effective adaptation to his or her business environment.

Consensus on the Need to Change

What we came to call "the Livonia Opportunity" was from its birth a process of industrial transformation rooted in the thinking of such pioneers as Likert, Maslow and McGregor, and supported by the quality of worklife process initiated by General Motors and the United Automobile Workers eight years earlier. The quality of worklife concept had been initially proposed to the corporation in 1970 by Irving Bluestone, then United Auto Workers vice president and director of the union's GM department.

> In the late 1960s I began making speeches and talking with people about the need for change. All management wanted was for workers to do a few jobs they taught them and not use their brains. I thought it was a tremendous waste. . . .

> Why should there have been objections and skepticism? Because the QWL process required that workers become involved in the decision-making process of the workplace. To some minds in management, this trespasses upon managerial prerogatives: . . . "What else are you going to give the union? Are you going to throw the keys away with the shop?"

> On the other side, union representatives also were very

reluctant . . . for fear that as workers became increasingly satisfied, they would have less loyalty to the union and this might erode the authority of the union and committeeman on the floor.

None of these things have come to pass[7]

With the gradual settling of fears and reluctance, an agreement between the UAW and General Motors was formalized in a letter of understanding, on November 19, 1973, establishing the UAW-GM National Committee to Improve the Quality of Work Life.

By 1980 roughly half of GM's plants had independently adopted some form of QWL activity with varying results, sometimes disappointing, sometimes encouraging.

The impending renovation of the Livonia plant was thus an opportunity to learn from the past and establish the best possible future, not as piecemeal change but as an *organic* function of a new operation: Livonia state-of-the-art plant.

It was clear to us from the start that effective transformation hinged on two key elements: **Our process had to be both integrated and comprehensive.**

An **integrated approach** would **balance** emphasis on a trio of objectives: quality, productivity and quality of worklife. The homey symbol of a three-legged milking stool came to exemplify our deep concern for a balanced approach at Livonia. Just as loss of a leg meant collapse, inattention or over attention to a single objective meant loss of the opportunity for lasting transformation. (The roads to transformation elsewhere have been dotted with scrapped programs that attempted to improve one of these three objectives at the expense of the others.) We liked the symbol of the milking stool enough to keep it and display it as a reminder of where we were headed.

A **comprehensive change** would involve multiple changes all consistent with and tied to one overall change process. Strong enough to overcome initial organization resistance and implemented such that the whole is greater than the sum of the parts.

Studies by Edward Lawler had already exposed the weaknesses of many unsuccessful programs for human resources development. "Off-the-shelf" programs failed when they (a) were implemented because of a fad ("quality circles" or "statistical quality control" *alone*, for example), (b) had no relationship to performance objectives, (c) were short-term, and (d) were not part of a comprehensive change. Fast on the heels of initial enthusiasm and good suggestions, such programs faced a sequence of hope for implementation, bitterness due to delay, a feeling that "no one was listening" and finally cynical questioning of management's effectiveness. Many programs were eventually dropped.[8]

Successful change, on the other hand, invariably worked when it was an element of comprehensive change embracing all of the interlocked areas within corporate life: quality systems, training, collective bargaining agreements, organization structure, compensation plans, work flow, communication and measurement systems, the physical plant environment and, fundamentally, the overall operating philosophy of the organization. Only comprehensive change is strong enough to overcome an organization's resistance to change.

It was clear from the start that integrated and comprehensive change was impossible without active union participation. It was time to regain our sight of the individual perceptions, motivations and aspirations of the workforce that would bring life to Livonia. It was time to revitalize the interpersonal bond between worker, supervisor, manager and union. The opening of Livonia was the opportunity to reestablish the sense of community, communication and participation in problem solving and decision making—both upline and downline—and its crucial effect on group cohesion and morale.

With all this in mind, and with the endorsement of UAW International's Irving Bluestone, the Livonia Opportunity began by involving Cadillac executives and top officials of UAW's local 22. Mr. Bluestone later commented:

> Truly successful endeavors in employee participation in decision-making are not developed by management and simply handed down to the union and the workforce. A successful improvement program derives from mutually agreed upon understandings in which the union and management are co-equal in planning, designing and implementing the employee involvement process . . . The Livonia Plant Project was born . . . as just such a joint effort. . . .
>
> It takes considerable courage and foresight for the representatives of management and of the union to break with tradition and move toward exciting and challenging new directions of work structure and work organization . . . We have embarked on such a course.[9]

The outcome of the Cadillac-UAW meetings was neither an official declaration nor a formal operating philosophy. Yet essential steps were taken. The meetings lead to a **required** consensus on the need to change.

Recognition of the need to change includes sponsoring a representative group of plant employees to examine the entire organization to find ways to meet future challenges. The group of plant people would analyze: objectives, expectations, structure, relationships, bargaining agreements, measurement systems, quality systems, etc.; formulate a comprehensive and integrated improvement plan; and seek approval of the plan from top company and union leadership.

Collaboration began as Cadillac and UAW Officials set initial broad objectives to guide plant employees . . .

- to build a high-quality product

- to improve our domestic and foreign competitive position

- to improve job security for Cadillac employees

- to provide the opportunity for employee involvement, development, and participation

- to establish a social system that complements the new technology

- to increase the amount of teamwork and job satisfaction for all Cadillac-Livonia employees

- to provide an example of Cadillac innovation to General Motors and the world

REVIEW/GUIDELINES/APPLICATION

TRANSFORMATION: STAGE 1

Consensus On The Need To Change

Transformation through an integrated and comprehensive process first requires some degree of change in how top company and union leaders perceive each other and behave toward one another. The extent of change needed will of course vary from one situation to another.

The attitude and behavior change follow recognition of the survival threat and realization of the need for a cooperative response. To help identify the nature and degree of needed change and the expected ease or difficulty of effecting it, you will need the answers to these questions:

- Who is the prime mover of the company? What are his or her responsibilities and authority?

- How flexible is this person in matters of company policy? relations with the union? relations with the workforce?

- Are this person's opinions and decisions respected by his or her colleagues? by the workforce?

- What degree of harmony or discord exists among the top management group? Are disagreements resolved easily?

- Who is the representative voice of the union? What are his or her responsibilities and authority?

- Are this person's opinions and decisions respected by other union leaders? by the union membership?

- How flexible is this person in discussions with management?

- What degree of harmony or discord has existed, and

exists now, between top management and the union? Are disagreements resolved easily?

- What are the basic beliefs of the leaders concerning the value of the workforce? How willing are they to listen and change?

Identification and verification of these variables through diagnosis is an important first step to a discussion of consensus on the need to change between management and the union. Depending on the existing culture, several steps with management separately and the union separately may be necessary before any joint activity is scheduled. Only when there is some agreement on basic values and the need to improve within the leadership of both groups, should they begin to meet together.

A suggested outline for one or more meetings between the top management group and the labor union leadership to obtain consensus.

1. *Arranging the meeting*

The ideal place to meet will be at a neutral site, away from both the business and union locations. This will help avoid interruptions, promote productive results and lend more significance to the meeting.

Both parties should allot enough time to assure in-depth analysis of the situation and adequate discussion—minimally, two days.

The meeting facilitator, chosen by consensus, should be trusted and respected by all participants, well versed in organization development techniques and able to generate productive thinking, creative solutions, participation, commitment and consensus. In most cases, a neutral outside consultant is in the best position to perform this role.

2. *Communication*

Initial tension between the two sides is natural. To move beyond this point the meeting facilitator should take advantage of structured group exercises designed to ease tension and encourage open communication[10].

3. *Historical background*

To fill in the sequence of events that have led to the need for the meeting, the facilitator should present, or arrange for someone else to present, a brief, concise history of developments in American business (see Chapter 1 of this book):

a) Growth during the 1950s and 1960s;

b) Productivity increases due to expanded U.S. markets and capital investment;

c) Maturity of U.S. markets in the 1970s; reliance on replacement markets; the oil crisis; "stagflation;"

d) The need for effective competition in worldwide markets;

e) Crisis of the 1980s: higher labor costs, quality problems, scarcity of capital, productivity stagnation and loss of markets due to intense foreign competition;

Transfer of high-volume, standardized production to developing countries with comparatively low wage rates; the concurrent emergence of Japanese and European industries with flexible systems and workforces adapted to high technology and skilled production.

Concessionary bargaining, low profits, reduced sales, high unemployment, diminishing union population, and, in many cases, plant closings and eventual bankruptcy.

f) The need for cooperation between the company and the union to upgrade quality, profitability and the worker's role and to assure job security and a fair share in profitability gain through jointly planned transformations.

g) The realities of the present situation: facing the option of continued management—union division or the development of a cooperative approach to generate sound economic health for the company and its workforce.

4. *Analysis of your organization*

Management and labor should explore together:

a) Where you now stand in terms of productivity, product quality, market growth, competitiveness, the quality of worklife and the present involvement and contributions of the workforce;

b) Where you want to be in five years;

c) The need for cooperative changes to ensure current stability and future growth.

5. *Recommendations*

Management and the union should now consider how best to approach a resolution, addressing these questions:

a) Do both sides agree on the need to change? If not, what issues are still left unsettled?

b) Are the two sides prepared to establish broad objectives for improvement? What is the most concise statement of these objectives?

c) Where is the ideal location (if there is a choice) to implement change? (Focus first on the strongest plants or departments.)

d) Discuss a procedure whereby a Planning Team—across-the-board representatives of the chosen plant or department—can analyze the entire plant or department and present a detailed plan of improvement for approval by the top management group and the labor union leaders.

e) Discuss the formation of this Planning Team, how its members are to be selected and how time is to be arranged and funds allocated to facilitate its effective operation.

(Development of a Planning Team is discussed in Chapter 4.)

Chapter 3

The Importance of Leadership

The Livonia engine plant—a facility of Cadillac Motor Car Division, General Motors Corporation—is located in Wayne County, Michigan, on Middlebelt Road just south of Highway I-96.

The original plant was built in 1971 as a satellite to the main machining operations in Detroit. Detroit machined the basic components of a cast-iron engine—blocks, cranks, intake manifolds and so on—and assembled and tested all current production engines. The Livonia operation was confined to machining a limited number of selected parts, with no assembling or engine testing. At the peak of joint operations, Detroit employed roughly 8,000 workers; Livonia managed with a relatively small workforce of about 400 people.

In 1979 the original Livonia operation was phased out to make way for a state-of-the-art plant that was designed and built as an extension of the old plant. Shortly before the changeover and the eventual shutdown of the old plant, only a small operating crew of about 50 people remained.

The new plant site, covering just over 38 acres, provided 1,000 parking spaces, conference rooms, a library/training room, a full-service cafeteria, rest areas on the plant floor and outdoor picnic areas.

The plant had the up-to-date technology, facilities, equipment, manufacturing processes and product design to produce a high-quality technologically advanced product: Cadillac's 4.1-liter, fuel-injected, aluminum block V-8 engine. Selected operations were computerized, governed by a central programmable computer that would allow monitoring and control of equipment and systems. Livonia's Statistical Process Control was the core of its quality philosophy—a system geared to the dimensional capabilities of a given machine operating under ideal conditions. By monitoring the machine's capability to produce a certain part (instead of monitoring blueprint tolerances for that part), we would be able to shut down and correct a wayward machine before it produced out-of-tolerance pieces. The system assisted us in consistently building engines right the first time.

In addition, the plant used automated operations and limited robotics to ease burdensome tasks and eliminate a number of mundane, repetitive jobs that are a normal part of any typical engine plant.

We now had a workplace to be proud of. Although it was no more exceptional than any number of similarly modern facilities in America and abroad designed within the past few years in various industries it was to us a major technological change. (The pure mechanics at Livonia presented a challenge to a high-seniority workforce used to outdated facilities. An aluminum block engine had never before been successfully produced in North America.) But, technological change aside, we were faced with the major tasks of developing the operating systems to bring the plant to life.

This was no run-of-the-mill plant: its broad objectives and the introduction of a dynamic new social system were neither traditional nor common to other "innovative" plants. In our response to the challenge to develop a plant that could compete in the global market and survive, we were about to launch a way of doing business that would depart radically from the average worker's perception of what was comfortably familiar and "secure" in the workplace.

Despite the depth of management's and the union's belief in what they were about to sponsor, the turning-point question was this: Would this relatively high-seniority salaried and hourly workforce be willing to adapt and restructure their worklives and replace old beliefs and relationships with new, more effective ones?

The answer would hinge largely on the strength of people at the plant level who would soon be chosen to plan and implement this major change. These hourly, union and management employees would fulfill the leadership role for the entire change process.

Unwavering leadership bound together by a common vision is essential to begin the transformation process. The strength of the leadership at the Livonia plant is best exemplified by the words plant level people **eventually** used in introducing the approved comprehensive change plan to the entire workforce.

To set the stage, the option to work at Livonia was offered to employees from the old machining operation in Detroit. We described the plant to our potential workforce, gave them the opportunity to tour Livonia, attend orientation sessions and ask questions before they decided to either join us or request placement elsewhere in the Cadillac organization.

We were not surprised that Livonia's physical environment impressed these people. Coming from a technologically outmoded facility—the hot, noisy, greasy workplace of a traditional machining operation—who would not be impressed by a state-of-the-art plant and a clean environment? But the seductive allure of computers, shiny new machines and a clean floor was a superficial attraction for these hardnosed realists. Their concerns were issues of job security and how changes would affect them individually.

They were worried about pay, seniority and transfer rights. They were fearful about the implications of fewer available jobs at Livonia. Coming from a traditionally adversarial environment, both salaried and hourly employees suspected management or the union of selling out. With their history of neglect, the workers were suspicious of an innovative social program, anxious about a changed hierarchy within the plant and wary of misplacing their trust. "Why should I believe you?" and "We've heard all this before!" were persistent—and understandable—responses at the orientation sessions.

Orientation meetings were difficult but the entire plan was presented to a skeptical workforce by a united front of management and union.

The gist of our message was this:

> It is true that Livonia will initially employ fewer people, both salaried and hourly. However, as we improve our quality and productivity, our costs will become more competitive, and our reputation for quality work will generate increased sales, greater customer loyalty and an expanded market. As the plant operation grows, we will be able to bring more people back to work.

> This is not going to happen overnight. It will take time. But job security for the greatest number of workers can only come from doing a better job right now and preparing ourselves for the future.

> We understand your skepticism. You have lived with a history of grievances, work stoppages and a difficult relationship with management. Until today you have had no evidence that management and the union can work together

toward a common objective, nor that they have been willing to do so.

For this, we have only one answer: We are trying to build a different kind of organization at Livonia. Talking alone will never convince you that this is so; we are going to have to demonstrate it. That demonstration can only come over time. We are asking you to give us the opportunity to prove that we mean what we say. This is an act of faith and we are asking you to accept us on those terms.

We want you to monitor us day by day. If neither management nor the union matches its actions to its words, then by all means you will have every right to complain. But you must give us the chance to prove that we are serious.

At the start some of you may have more to lose than others. But in the long run we will all be better off. Our industry has had a history of layoffs and plant closings. Your present status doesn't mean a thing if you are out of work, and can't pay the rent. Holding on to the traditional way of running things doesn't mean a thing if you can't feed your family.

We don't have all the answers and we don't even know all the questions. This is so because, for the first time, we are not handing you a cut-and-dried program; what happens at Livonia will happen because we are going to come together to create it for ourselves. The changes embodied in our overall improvement plan constitute nothing more than a starting point and an initial framework to help us begin to move in a new direction.

We are going to make mistakes, but they will be mistakes that grow out of an honest mutual effort to build a social system that works for everyone in this room, that gives each of us the chance to be involved productively and to participate meaningfully in the work we do together.

We are not interested in piecemeal innovations that look slick but go nowhere. We want innovations that are a part of a comprehensive program of real change. We are interested only in that kind of profound change—involving every aspect or our jobs—that will transform our work lives and our personal lives.

The broad objectives born of the Cadillac-United Auto

Workers meetings and the resulting plan of transformation was the product of a balanced group representing the union, management and the hourly workforce: a cohesive Planning Team of equals working together. This is not a ''program'' drawn up by one faction and dictated to the others.

A modern plant and committed leadership can break no new ground without a cooperative effort and the support of a dedicated and continually improving workforce.

Although a small number of workers questioned their ability to adapt and another fraction rejected employment outright, 88% of those offered the opportunity to join us at Livonia accepted.

Why was the eventual plan so roundly accepted? An essential element was that the local leadership was up to the task at hand. The plan was the final product of the crucially important nucleus of transformation called the **Planning Team**. This team was selected after top leadership from the company and union agreed on the need to change and established overall objectives.

REVIEW/GUIDELINES/APPLICATION

TRANSFORMATION: STAGE 2

Leadership

Comprehensive change from the traditional to the innovative is an uncertain and problematic process. It is a contest between advocates of "leave things as they are" and those who believe that significant change for the better—no matter how challenging that process may be—is worth the effort to effect that change.

The need for change becomes a pressing issue when survival, or even the continued sound economic health of an organization is at stake.

To meet the conditions of the contest—for it is often a direct confrontation between the reactionary and visionary forces within a company—those who lead must have a clear, purposeful, sustained, fundamental belief in the necessity and rightness of cooperative enterprise: that management, labor unions and workers can join together, working toward a common objective, to create a productive, long-lasting partnership.

Although support from the highest echelons of the company and its workers' union is essential, it is most often the leadership at the plant level who must take the reins and act as prime movers for productive change. Since it is the rare organization that will be blessed with ideal leaders, effective transformation within most companies will depend on people who **are capable of creating within themselves**, most of these leadership qualities:

- credibility, to foster trust among others
- a foundation of fairness and honesty in all relationships within the organization
- the ability to listen openly and completely—that is, without prejudgment or false solicitude
- a sense of purpose, and a capacity for consistency of word and action

- the ability to participate fully with colleagues upline and downline

- the willingness to bypass vested interests that may be detrimental to the common goal

- the strength to resist peer pressure and unfounded accusations while understanding the reasons for their existence

- a sense of one's own worth, technical competence, strengths and weaknesses, and the willingness to act in appropriate measure to those qualities

- the ability to perceive positive qualities in others, and the willingness to delegate responsibilities in a measure appropriate to those qualities

- the willingness to admit mistakes and errors of judgment, and the readiness to correct them quickly and openly

- the willingness and ability to learn, adapt and grow hand in hand with the rest of the organization

Because a leader is a model of direction and action, and the workforce a reflection of that visible leadership, the success or failure of comprehensive change rests squarely upon those men and women ready to guide and teach by personal example. Strength will beget strength, and belief will beget belief; toward these ends, there are no shortcuts or magic formulas.

Chapter 4

THE PLANNING TEAM/PART 1
Getting Started

Following the consensus on the need to change and developing a
statement of broad objectives, selection of the Planning Team is
company and union leadership's first important step in passing the
baton of transformation to plant level employees. This group will
function as a "critical mass" in the process of change—that is, as a
closely bonded nucleus with the power to attract others, to grow, and
thus widen that attraction in all directions.

The Planning Team is the group empowered to analyze the entire
organization, solve problems and make decisions in order to develop
an improvement plan appropriate to the organization. It is an autonomous group, responsible for promoting and implementing an approved plan at the plant level, to embrace over time the entire
workforce. The only constraint on the Planning Team is that top
company and union leadership must approve its plan prior to implementation.

Who is on the Planning Team?

To be fully effective the Planning Team must represent every
department, group, and faction within the organization—**without
exception**—that will be affected by its plan of comprehensive change.
At Livonia this meant representatives of the union, the hourly work-

force, and skilled trades (a key sub-group within the hourly work-force); the plant manager; responsible representatives from the departments of personnel, finance, plant production management, material management, quality control, plant engineering, and process engineering; and, finally, an overall administrator to facilitate the work of the Planning Team.

In addition, the selection process at Livonia took care—as this process should do in all organizations—to assure a fair representation of a cross-section of the company's population, including minority groups, female employees, and workers from both high and low seniority groups.

The size of the Planning Team will of course depend on the dimensions of the organization it represents. Once a level of total representation is reached, however, the group should be confined to a manageable size. Although organizational research indicates that a seven member group is optimal, we have found that a group size of from twelve to sixteen members is within practical limits. (The Livonia Planning Team consisted of fifteen people.)

What qualities do we want in the Planning Team?

No thinking person will voluntarily follow an inept, deceitful, or irresponsible leader. Nor will he or she willingly follow the guidance of a leadership group that appears purposeless, manipulative, or hypocritical.

If a leader or leading group is to guide others through a simple task or through an easily assimilated or minor process of no great challenge, then the qualities of leadership are not terribly important, however desirable they may be in the abstract. But if the task or process is problematic, demanding, and involves significant change from traditional practice, the qualities of leadership are supremely important.

The latter is precisely the situation facing the Planning Team: It must function as a serious and dedicated model of thought and behavior, as a cohesive "critical mass" at the core of the thorny process of organizational transformation.

For this reason the top management group and the labor union leadership must exercise wisdom and care in its selection of those who will form the Planning Team. No candidate is an "automatic" choice, regardless of his or her position, until his or her qualities have been cautiously assessed to match the task ahead. Nor should someone be selected with the thought that "Oh, he'll come around in time," as an excuse for selection. If, on the other hand, management and labor cannot agree on candidates strongly favored by one side or the other, then they should engage a respected independent third party to conduct assessments and help make final selection decisions.

What qualities do we look for?

The willingness to participate: Whenever possible, membership should be voluntary. This eliminates, or at least minimizes, the likelihood of jeopardizing the group's work because of resentment, a defeatist attitude, or a demoralizing influence.

Depending on the talent freely available, however, the top leadership (the selection committee) may have to resort to organizational changes in order to move responsive individuals into departments that might otherwise go unrepresented on the Planning Team. Although this is the least desirable approach to fair and adequate representation, the leadership, having already reached a consensus on the need to change, may have no other choice. The stakes are too high to allow defeat at this crucial stage.

The selection committee may also face outright rejection by a favored candidate. At Livonia, for instance, the first union representative selected refused on the basis that "the process was just a design by management to get more out of the employees." (This person currently works at Livonia and has become a strong supporter of its program of change.)

Credibility within one's own department: This quality is crucial, not only in dealings with one's immediate colleagues but in all relationships. Needless to say it is essential for a Planning Team member who wishes to share information, opinions, and suggestions for action with those he or she represents, with the intention of inspiring confidence in a non-traditional point of view.

A progressive attitude, coupled with strength of purpose: The process of organizational transformation is, as we have already said, often a direct confrontation between the reactionary and visionary forces within a company. To make that process work those on the leading edge of change must bring this belief to their task: that a change for the better is desirable, possible, and worth the effort to overcome barriers to its successful realization.

Transformation moves from values to vision, attitudes, and finally to changed behavior. Planning Team members should subscribe to the following basic values:

- Employees have unique expertise about their job;

- Most employees want to and are able to contribute to the success of the organization;

- Employees want to have input into decisions affecting their jobs and lives;

- Appropriate involvement leads to better decisions and better results;

- Individual growth and development is both an organizational objective and essential in order to achieve other organizational objectives.

Our experience at Livonia made it plain that great pains should be taken to avoid staffing mistakes. One member can single-handedly undermine a team effort; and removal of a disruptive member, once the group has begun its work, unnecessarily drains away time, team energy and a sense of cohesiveness.

This is not to imply that the chosen group will be a team of 100% boosters or lighthearted enthusiasts! It is closer to the truth to acknowledge that the selection committee and the team facilitator will be faced with seven or twelve or fifteen anxious and wary individuals who will not fully understand their mission!

The Role of the Planning Team Facilitator

The facilitator's job is to turn this newly formed collection of individuals into an enlightened, well-trained, and mutually supportive team. To replace tension with trust, disbelief with understanding and division with a sense of common purpose, the facilitator must establish a common meeting ground for this array of diverse attitudes, preconceptions, and vested interests. Only then will the Planning Team understand fully the nature and importance of its task. The person empowered with this responsibility must be trusted by all participants.

To accomplish these goals the facilitator must have first-class skills in group development, problem solving and decision making. He or she is also responsible for the logistics of the group meetings, including initial organization of the sessions, and their scheduling, preparation and agenda.

Some organizations may be fortunate enough to have such a person already on staff. In most cases, however, the company will have to engage a professional consultant to fill this role. But under no circumstances should the management-union leadership underestimate the vital importance of the facilitator's function and qualifications. To "make-do" with a less-than-skilled employee, simply to avoid an expense, is to undermine the transformation process at the start. (Details about Livonia's choice, and what this entailed, are described in a later section of this book.)

Time and money

The Planning Team, working hand in hand with its facilitator, must have time to function properly. This means that the top leadership must work out a schedule that allots adequate time for team development—**on company time**—without disrupting plant operations.

Participation in the Livonia team required *over half* of its members' working time for about one year. This may appear to have been a drain on our time resources, but it was not. We planned carefully and initiated effective job coverage, permitting both normal plant operations and unhindered Planning Team activities. Subsequent projects indicate that the Planning Team can effectively accomplish its task over four to six months.

How a company allocates its employees' time is a matter of priorities. If the goal of transformation is seen as a clear imperative, a workable schedule is always possible. On the other hand a "business as usual" attitude coupled with a low priority for Planning Team development will kill transformation at its roots, and every preparatory step will have been a foolish waste of time.

How we spend company money is also a matter of priorities. A full-time, on-site professional facilitator is expensive. It is also expensive to take employees off the job to participate in Planning Team activities. Training programs cost money, and additional funding will be needed as team development progresses.

A budget-conscious company will balk at talk of added expenses, but it should also consider the alternatives: What is the cost of lost productivity? of layoffs? of plant closing? of possible bankruptcy? What dollar value will we place on job security, on sound economic health and on the life of the organization itself? Looked at in perspective (is there any other way?), the relatively small investment in Planning Team development is clearly a manageable necessity.

For Livonia's large industrial operation, covering a workforce of 1,200 people, the direct investment in the planning team was about $40,000. Orientation and training for the entire workforce was considerably more expensive; however, even this expense was insignificant compared to the investment in capital improvements and resulting improved performance.

As a result of this investment, we saw **in one year's time** fundamental changes in our physical environment, organizational structure, operating systems and procedures, decision-making and problem-solving processes, and company-wide communications and measurement networks.

During the first two years of production we witnessed major improvements in product quality, productivity, and employee interaction, loyalty, and participation. Steady improvement has continued for five years.

- Product quality as measured by conformance to specifications moved to within a few tenths of a percentage point of perfection and consistently remained at that high level.

- Customer complaints dropped by 40%, and warranty claims by 56% in the first year and an additional 39% in the second year.

- Assembly and test discrepancies dropped by 75%.

- Daily production increased by over 100% by the end of the first year, and leaped another 25% in the second year.

- Machine uptime increased by 33%.

- Actual controllable costs per engine built were reduced by 50%, including labor, burden and overtime premiums, with a 37% drop in scrap alone in the first year and 22% in the second year (1st to 2nd year average).

- We witnessed a 10% improvement in housekeeping ratings, a 23% reduction in injuries and a 50% drop in absenteeism.

- Employee suggestions improved by several hundred percent, both in frequency and for their dollar savings to the company.

- By all realistic measurements, employee grievances practically disappeared: The number filed in one year at Livonia equalled what one could expect **in one week** in a traditional plant of comparable size. In addition, with a few exceptions, the grievances filed were all settled at the plant level.

As a Return On Investment of time and money in workforce

development and training, these are visible, measurable results. Not so neatly measurable, however, are the far more fundamental changes that result in unstinting organizational support of, belief in, and commitment of people empowered to initiate significant change for the better.

It is this combination of investments that make real the potential power and practical results of an eminently workable process of positive transformation.

REVIEW/GUIDELINES/APPLICATION

TRANSFORMATION: STAGE 3

The Planning Team: A "Critical Mass"

The Planning Team is the organization's bridge between the management-labor union leadership and the workforce. Once selected, trained, and enlightened, it will function autonomously to design, promote, and implement an approved plan at the plant level. In this sense it can be thought of as a "critical mass," a cohesive nucleus of change that will over time form the central core of comprehensive transformation throughout the organization.

The effectiveness of the Planning Team depends on several factors:

1. Its members must represent **every** department, group, and faction within the organization, and must reflect a cross-section of the company's population.

2. Its members must be trusted, credible, and progressive.

3. Its members must believe that change for the better is desirable, possible, and worth any effort to overcome barriers to its successful realization.

4. Its members must believe in basic values concerning employee development and participation.

5. Its members must be prepared to communicate the purpose, value, and necessity of its plan to the entire workforce, demonstrating those qualities by personal example.

It is more than probable that the selected group, despite the qualifications of its members, will bring disbelief, anxiety, misconceptions, and a misunderstanding of its mission to the first meeting. It is the task of a Planning Team Facilitator to replace these negative qualities with trust, understanding, and a sense of common purpose.

The facilitator, faced with an enormously responsible role, must be fully equipped to build an effective, cohesive, and mutually supportive team. In most cases the organization must turn to an outside professional consultant trained in group development and the techniques of problem solving and decision making. A person with lesser skills should not be considered, despite the expense of additional staffing.

At this point in the transformation process, the top leadership must carefully review its priorities. Adequate time to function and adequate funding for its development must be allocated to the Planning Team. Skimping on either time or money will undermine the process of change at its most vulnerable stage. Since the Planning Team cannot function without a trained facilitator, the cost of this professional—who should be engaged as a full-time, on-site team member—must also be met.

The expenses of divided employee time, probable extra job coverage, and all needs related to Planning Team development and training must be viewed within the perspective of the company's present condition, its projection of future growth, and the negative factors of reduced productivity, possible layoffs, plant closings, and the bankruptcy that follows severe business losses.

If the goal of transformation is seen as a clear imperative, the issues of time and funding priorities become clearer, and the organization will better understand the necessity for full support of and an open-handed commitment to Planning Team development.

Chapter 5

THE PLANNING TEAM/PART 2

Orientation

At this stage the selected group of seven or twelve or fifteen individuals is a "planning team" in name only. Its members have, at best, only the scantest notion of the team missions, and possess neither the skills, wisdom, nor perspective to take on and successfully complete any significant work.

At this point the team facilitator, in cooperation with the management-union leadership, must launch the group's three-stage preparation of orientation, training and enlightenment—a kind of high-level corporate "boot camp" to raise the trainees to a level of broad intelligence and sharp-edged efficiency consistent with their future mission, a set of three sequential objectives:

- to develop an overall operating **philosophy** for the organization
- to develop an overall operating **plan** appropriate to that philosophy
- to develop the steps required to **implement** the operating plan at the plant level

We cannot overstate the necessity for the most thorough team preparation, however long that may take. As any building will collapse if its underpinnings are neither sunk deep enough nor built strong enough to support the weight and strain of its superstructure, organizational transformation will almost certainly fail if team preparation is thinned out, cut short, or otherwise neglected. The common paths to failure include (among other likely traps) corporate enthusiasm that runs high at the outset, only to deflate over time, and the understandable rush to "get the job done at any cost"—when "at any cost" means shallow training, with its inevitable consequences: fragile, ill-conceived, premature, inappropriate and unsupported plans of action.

A full-dress three-stage preparation is therefore a *must* if the Planning Team is to possess the understanding, wisdom, perspective, knowledge, experience and reasoning capabilities consistent with its mission.

Orientation

The orientation sessions give the team its first opportunity to understand the purpose, urgency, and seriousness of its mission, and to learn how it will accomplish this task. Through free give-and-take, it is also a time to have preconceptions, misunderstandings, apprehensions, and all unanswered questions aired, discussed openly and moved toward resolution.

Given the nature of traditional American business operations ("Management leads; workers follow"), the opening orientation session is an historic event for the organization: the first meeting between the top management-union leadership and a handful of people given the mandate, as equals, to shape the company's future. Company and union leaders must communicate, in plain and forthright language, the events that have led to the meeting, the urgency of the mandate for change, and a true picture of its expectations and visions. The agenda, in short, must be a dynamic re-run, with appropriate amplification, of those early meetings that produced top management's and the labor union leadership's consensus on the need to change:

- a review of American business cycles from the 1950s to the present time

- an analysis of the organization's current status, where present conditions are likely to take the company in future years, and the disparity between that reality and a vision of what is possible

- the need for a joint and cooperative effort among all affected groups in the organization
- a presentation of broad objectives, as drawn up by a united management-union leadership
- how and why the members of the Planning Team were chosen
- a discussion of how the Planning Team will function to develop an overall operating philosophy, an overall operating plan, and the steps to implement that plan at the plant level
- a statement of corporate support for the team's cooperative effort to improve organizational effectiveness, underlining the group's autonomy in suggesting changes in all areas touching operations, policy, and agreements

As broad-based and free-swinging as this agenda may be, each aspect must be given its due, presented with frankness and discussed in open forum. The team's responsibilities to itself and to the leadership must be made clear: the Planning Team's autonomy in developing an overall plan and the leadership's need to approve that plan.

The agenda touches on dynamic issues that invite discussion, serious questioning, and controversy. But it is toward the full airing of response, the clear answers to legitimate questions, and the resolution of differences that this fundamental orientation must address itself.

As diligent as all first-session participants may be, not all issues will have been discussed to the satisfaction of all team members. This is the reason for a follow-up meeting between the Planning Team and its facilitator.

At this separate session he or she will review and clarify these points:

1. Responsibilities

"All of you have been challenged with a major responsibility to the organization and everyone in it.

"Your job will be to design a total operating philosophy and plan with a double objective. What you develop must satisfy the company's need for bottom-line results (improved quality, increased productivity). But, at the same time, it must fulfill the needs of its people for a genuine sense of individual achievement and personal recognition.

"Everything you do must be rooted in the honest belief that, given the proper foundation and environment, American management, labor unions, and workers can pull together to outperform any industrial team in the world.

"In short, we have to put our traditional adversarial relationships behind us for the first time and find a better way to get along."

2. Leadership

"The management and union leadership have a vision they have just shared with you. However, they can't realize this vision without your help. They are asking you to be leaders in creating the blueprint for change.

"How you think and act, what you believe, and how you communicate with others will now affect everyone in the organization. The entire company, over time, will become a reflection of your visible leadership.

"A good leader has certain qualities. Not the least of these qualities is the ability to meet and overcome the stumbling blocks, barriers, and criticism that others will put in your path. Change is difficult for many of your co-workers. Until they fully understand what you are trying to do, you won't win any popularity contests. If you accept that and understand that your goal is to improve the quality of their lives and secure their future, you will do a better job."

3. Autonomy

"No one is going to tell you what to do or how to do it. You will be free to examine every aspect of this organization, to question how things are done, and to suggest a better way of doing them.

"Because we are a team, we have built-in checks and balances. Everyone here will listen to your opinions, and you will listen to theirs. We will air our differences until we have reached a consensus on whatever the topic may be.

"Despite our autonomy there will be areas that are outside the framework of our missions. We will discuss these issues when they come up. But until they do you have the right and obligation to focus on the organization as a totality. Only after we develop an entire plan will we require approval and authorization to proceed with implementation."

4. Time and money

"From now on, part of your time will be spent at your regular job and part in Planning Team training and activities. Everything you do will continue to be on company time, and you will be paid accordingly.

"From time to time our team activities may involve extra hours, especially for outside tours of other plant facilities. The company will cover all expenses; however, there will be no overtime pay for time spent travelling."

5. Training

"We know that many of you may feel unprepared to handle this job. It is obviously a big task that has to be done right.

"But you have been selected because management and the union feel that you are the kind of people who can grasp the enormous importance of this mission and be receptive to the extensive training we will give you to accomplish it.

"You will be trained in problem-solving and decision-making techniques, and—because our mission is so closely bound to the daily lives of our co-workers and the quality of their worklife—you will be instructed in the study of human behavior and behavorial sciences.

"For now, however, our objectives as a team are personal development, understanding, and the establishment of trust and commitment."

REVIEW/GUIDELINES/APPLICATION

TRANSFORMATION: STAGE 4

Orientation Of The Planning Team

Orientation gives the newly formed Planning Team a basic understanding of the purpose, urgency, and seriousness of its mission, and how it will accomplish that task.

Until the three-stage process of orientation, training, and enlightenment is completed, the team is unprepared to do significant work toward its eventual objectives. These goals are the development of an overall operating philosophy, a plan of action consistent with that philosophy and the practical steps required to implement the plan at the plant level.

Full preparation, beginning with the comprehensive orientation, is a *must*. Without it, the team's work will be pointless and organizational transformation a practical impossibility.

A suggested outline for the first orientation session(s)

Participants:
(a) top management
(b) labor union leadership
(c) Planning Team Facilitator
(d) Planning Team

Number of sessions:
One or more, as needed

Meeting place:
At the discretion of the leadership, although a neutral site, away from both the business and union locations, is preferable.

Time:
All participants should allot enough time to assure in-

depth analysis of the situation, and time for questions, answers, and discussions.

Homework:
Questions for the leadership group:

Do you know the name of the team facilitator, and his or her background and credentials?

Do you know the name of each member of the Planning Team, and his or her position in the organization or union?

What do you know about the character and reputation of each team member? If you had not met him or her prior to the selection process, have you learned something about this person prior to the orientation session?

Do you have a clear sense of the agenda and objectives of the first session with the Planning Team?

Questions for the team facilitator and the Planning Team:

Do you know the names and positions of those in the top management group and the labor union leadership?

Are you familiar with their areas of responsibility, the work they've done, and their positions on various issues that have affected the quality of worklife in your industry?

Are you prepared to set aside, or help others set aside, any preconceptions that may interfere with open communication at the orientation sessions?

Agenda:

The spokesperson(s) for the leadership group should be prepared to present a clear, concise, and honest picture of the events that have led to the decision to form and empower the Planning Team. These statements, addressed to the Planning Team, should answer the following questions:

    (a) What has been going on in American industry over the past three decades? See Chapters 1-2 of this book.

(b) Where does our company stand today in terms of productivity, quality work, growth and its share of the market?

(c) Continuing as we are now, what are our prospects for the future?

(d) How do these realistic prospects match our hopes for the organization's future?

(e) What have been the consequences of our (management/labor/union/workforce) traditional roles as adversaries?

(f) Why and how did the management-union leadership reach a consensus on the need to change this traditional relationship?

(g) As a result of this consensus, what broad objectives have we agreed on?

(h) What is the link between these objectives and our decision to form a Planning Team?

(i) Why and how were you (the team members) selected? What qualities were we looking for?

(j) How do we visualize your role in the process of change? What do we expect you to do, and how do we expect you to do it?

(k) What kind of support can you expect from us?

(l) Are there any aspects of what we've presented that you would like clarified?

A suggested outline for the follow-up orientation session(s)

Participants:
(a) Planning Team Facilitator
(b) Planning Team

Number of sessions:
One or more, as needed.

Meeting place:
As we said earlier the facilitator is responsible for the logistics of the group meetings. This follow-up session is an ideal time to establish a fixed in-plant location that is

convenient for the team members, comfortable to work in and situated in a place that minimizes distractions and interruptions.

Time:

At the discretion of the facilitator but with the prior agreement of team members.

Homework:

Questions for the team facilitator:

Do you have a clear sense of the agenda and objectives of this session?

Have you kept reference notes about the first session(s), detailing both settled and controversial issues, and the specific responses of the team members?

Are you prepared to clarify unsettled issues and answer the comments, questions, and objections these may have raised?

Questions for the Planning Team:

For issues that have not been resolved to your satisfaction, have you prepared specific comments, questions, or objections?

Are you prepared to set aside, or help others set aside, any prejudices or fixed positions that may interfere with open communication at the follow-up session?

Agenda:

This is a pivotal meeting. Although its immediate purpose is to review and clarify issues presented earlier by the management-union leadership, it will also establish a model for all future meetings between the Planning Team and its facilitator.

A well run session will help establish a close rapport among all its participants, create opportunities for mutual trust and personal commitment, and identify the gathering as a "safe place" where members can speak their mind in a forum where open communication is encouraged and respected.

At this time the facilitator should make a balanced presentation. He or she may choose to pass quickly over issues that have caused no special comment, permitting more time for those that are clearly unsettled or appear controversial. **In all cases, however, he or she must invite comments and questions and allow the meeting to flow naturally and democratically.**

The basic topics should include responsibilities, leadership, autonomy, time and money and training, more or less following the guidelines outlined on previous pages.

Orientation is over when the group, even at this early stage, understands its mission, the specific role it will play in the improvement process, its rights and responsibilities, its limitations and the steps it will take to accomplish its task.

Chapter 6

Managing a Team Development Process

A newly-oriented Planning Team is a collection of strong individuals pulling in various directions. They must be aligned so that they can strive together to achieve a common purpose. A three-phase skill development and team building process is necessary to begin alignment and assist the facilitator to fashion an effective Planning Team.

The first phase of the program teaches **basic skills**: instruction in problem solving and decision making, the study of behavioral science principles, and the study of organizational resistance to change.

The second phase is a formal **team building** activity designed to bond members into a close-knit unit, and to identify operating norms and principles—that is, **how** Planning Team members will work together to accomplish their mission.

The third phase of the development program is concerned with the Planning Team's **enlightenment**. Experiences at this stage give the team an awareness of what is possible: the awareness goes beyond the organization it serves by exposing the planners to the accomplishments of other plants and industries.

PHASE ONE: (a) Problem solving and decision making

The wholesale reevaluation of an organization (its policies, structure, operations, and so on) is obviously a formidable job. Anyone, or any group, attempting to take on the challenge **with the hopes of a successful outcome** must be skilled in **rational** approaches to the four kinds of questions managers ask every day:[11]

> **What's going on?**
> **Why did this happen?**
> **Which course of action should we take?**
> **What lies ahead?**

- **"What's going on?"** begs for clarification, a sorting out, a breaking down, a key to the map of current events, a means of achieving and maintaining control. It reflects the pattern of thinking that enables us to impose order where all had been confusion.

  Situation Appraisal—a rational process based on this thinking pattern—is a tool to cut down time and energy wasted on misunderstanding and misuse of information. It is the starting point for any effective team action, leading us to take more productive actions more often by setting priorities rationally and paying precise attention to appropriate answers.

- **"Why did this happen?"** indicates the need for **cause-and-effect** thinking, a pattern linked to rational processes called Problem Analysis and Performance Analysis.

  Problem Analysis enables a group to accurately identify, describe, analyze, and resolve a situation in which **something has gone wrong without explanation.** Performance Analysis provides the same tools to analyze human performance problems.

- **"Which course of action should we take?"** implies that some choice must be made based on a determination of our purpose, our consideration of available options, and our assessment of the relative risks or productivity of those options.

  Decision Analysis—the rational process based on the choice-making pattern of thinking—provides the decision maker with a basis for saying what is to be preferred on balance with all things considered. Its single greatest advantage for the organization may be that it provides a common language and approach that removes decision making from the realm of personal, idiosyncratic behavior.

- **"What lies ahead?"** reflects a thinking pattern that enables us to look into the future to imagine the good and bad it may hold. Potential Problem Analysis is the rational process based on our concern with what **might** be and what **could** happen. It uses what we know or can safely assume in order to avoid possible negative consequences in the future. It is a positive search for ways to avoid and lessen trouble, providing individuals and organizations with their best chance to build the future in accordance with their visions and desires.

In time the Livonia Planning Team would return again and again to the rational processes in which it had been trained. Formation of the original overall operating plan, for example, with all of the required solutions, decisions, and modifications, relied heavily on these processes. Without them the team would almost certainly have wasted energy in fruitless debate.

PHASE ONE: (b) Behavioral science principles

Training in the hows and whys of human behavior gives the Planning Team the insight it will need to design systems and operations **that work with real people in real industrial situations**.

The team must understand why people act as they do; how behavior is affected by organizational systems and the work environment; the dynamics of human motivations and expectations, the impact of changes and so on.

To avoid the pitfall of "reinventing the wheel," team members must also become lay historians in the areas of applied social psychology and organization development. In short **they must know what has already happened!** This important study includes for example, Frederick Taylor's "scientific management," Rensis Likert's work in human resources and workgroups, Abraham Maslow's theories of motivation and needs, Douglas MacGregor's study of human relations in the modern organization and the like.

Linked with such foundational work are the elements, successes, and failures found in modern industrial experimentation: what went on in Sweden, at the Saab and Volvo plants; profit sharing approaches (such as the Scanlon Plan); designs for worker participation; the concept of "situational management;" flexible manufacturing systems popularized by the Japanese—in effect, all past work that in any way touches on the nature of the Planning Team's mission.

This framework of knowledge, understanding and perspective, working hand in hand with the rational processes, will assist the Planning Team to develop alternatives that assure a performance level consistent with the organization's overall objectives. To approach the task in any lesser way—perhaps, at worst, with a "let's do it and hope for the best" attitude—would be folly indeed.

PHASE ONE: (c) Organizational resistance to change

Selling would be child's play if every customer smiled broadly, grabbed our hand in delight, and said, "Great! Of course I'll buy!" Unfortunately, no product or plan, however "perfect," will ever get that degree of acceptance we dream of!

In order to design, sell, and implement its improvement plan—no matter how "ideal" or "good for them" the group may deem it—the Planning Team must understand and be prepared to overcome resistance to change.

Resistance will come from every corner of the organization:

- **workers asked to change their behavior**
  Existing expectations, selection systems, reward, sanctions and so on, mold specific behavior patterns. Resistance to change occurs when these old patterns are at odds with behavioral changes required by new organizational systems.

- **specialists threatened by change**
  Organizational changes may be perceived as threats to the expertise and prestige of specialized groups. For example, the elimination of traditional pay classifications is seen as an erosion of the skilled worker's standing in the labor community.

- **those in positions of power or authority**
  As the power structure within an organization is equalized through structural changes, and as the workforce is given greater autonomy, people formerly in positions of authority (assigned, evolved, or imagined) will be among the first to resist those changes.

- **people who are exploiting the status quo**
  Organizational change will be seen by some as a threat-

ening situation that "rocks the boat" of traditional work practices. Their resistance to change will be in direct proportion to the degree by which these changes expose inadequacies or shortcomings within, or manipulation of, the company's former systems and structure.

One of the most effective approaches to anticipated resistance taught to and used by the Livonia Planning Team is a tool labeled "force field analysis." Using this procedure the team analyzes a given change in terms of (a) **driving forces** that push for implementation of the change, and (b) **restraining forces** that resist implementation of the change. Successful implementation is facilitated, then, by an appropriate adjustment of these opposing forces: (a) by increasing the driving forces through newly designed operating systems and procedures; or (b) by removing enough of the restraining forces to ease the forward movement; or (c) through a sensitive rebalancing of **both** driving and restraining forces.

(Later in this book we detail a number of the specific changes recommended by the Livonia Planning Team and the processes surrounding their approval and eventual implementation. One of these— "The Case of the General Foreman"—is an especially valuable illustration of how "force field analysis" was put to work to resolve a sensitive and pivotal issue.)

PHASE TWO: Team building experience

By this time the Planning Team members should be reasonably comfortable with one another and will have grown naturally into a higher degree of mutual trust. The purpose of team building experiences is to enhance these beginnings by increasing the group's comfort level and its sense of confidence as a team, to bond its individuals into a tightly knit, mutually supportive working body, and to help the group reach a consensus on how it will go about its task.

Here the job of the facilitator or a trained consultant is to involve the team in structured experiences designed to remove barriers to trust and open communication. This process was explained at Livonia through the use of the "Johari Window," a model used to illuminate the importance of self-disclosure and feedback in building interpersonal relationships. (This classic model is fully described at the end of this chapter.)

As a result of work of this sort the Livonia team members clearly shifted to a higher level of interaction. Everyone was more willing to express ideas openly and more receptive to feedback from the rest of the team. As one person (an hourly worker) commented, "When we began I thought it was a joke. I didn't think **anything** would change, and I didn't know why I was chosen. Now I believe we can do it and I have something to contribute."

The Planning Team's discussion of its operating norms and principles was largely based on its refreshed perception of itself, on its awareness of the value of group decisions (the result of other exercises) and on an appreciation of the strength of the group **working as a team**. From here it was an easy step for the Livonia team to reach conclusions on how they would work together:

- that each member was free to express any idea about any topic under discussion

- that all ideas, comments, and suggestions would be fully aired and evaluated

- that all decisions would be made by consensus only

PHASE THREE: Enlightenment

The purpose of the "enlightenment" phase of the development process is to expose the Planning Team members to current, real world approaches and alternatives **previously unknown to them**. For such an exploration to make any sense, however, this "trip into foreign waters" has a substantial prerequisite: the team must proceed from **a thorough working knowledge** of its own company's product, existing manufacturing and quality control processes, current technology, criteria for performance measurement, past and present performance data, and projections of future performance—a comprehensive imperative, all of this! For it is only with this breadth of preparedness that the Planning Team will be armed to evaluate what it finds, ask the right questions, seek the best answers, and place its discoveries in proper perspective.

To get a real sense of what is going on "out there," nothing replaces first-hand observation and face-to-face talks with people working out their problems in other organizations. With these goals in mind the Livonia Planning Team, now fully ready for its "enlightenment" phase, used decision analysis techniques to select other innovative General Motors plants to visit.

Using previously learned decision analysis techniques, the Planning Team first identified objectives desired in a tour site.

Objectives

- Plants that were innovative and not traditional
- Plants where an improvement plan was operational
- Plants where the workforce is represented by a union
- Plant populations similar to Livonia
- Plants with existing high seniority workforce
- Plants that improved using a technology or product similar to Livonia
- Plants that incorporated improved measures of quality, productivity and quality of worklife
- Ability to see teams in operation while on tour
- Ability to talk to a variety of people while on tour
- Computer monitoring systems in the plant

Working with these objectives the Planning Team evaluated fifteen plant sites and selected three alternatives: Delco Electronics in Albany, Georgia; Packard Electric plant in Warren, Ohio; and Rochester Carburetor in Tuskaloosa, Alabama.

The Albany Delco Electronics plant, a unionized facility, worked within an innovative team concept, using a pay-for-knowledge compensation system, an assessment center for selection of salaried employees, computer-controlled maintenance functions, and a quick-start training program for hourly employees.

The Packard Electric facilities were designed by a joint union-management committee faced with a crisis of lost jobs. Selection of the Warren plant allowed the team to tour three new plant sites that had few job classifications and had transferred an existing workforce to a new facility.

The Rochester Carburetor plant was a recently unionized facility using innovative pay-for-knowledge compensation techniques in a team approach to production and assembly. The Tuscaloosa plant had only one skilled trade classification and used an assessment center for selecting employees to open the plant.

Following selection of the plant sites, the Planning Team members developed a list of more than 150 questions that they would ask during the tour. Reviewing some of the questions will demonstrate the type of information that can be gathered by visiting other plants.

A. History of Improvement Process
1. Why was the program started? By whom?
2. What is the overall mission?
3. When was the program first started?
4. What was the time frame for completion?
5. Was it a joint union/management decision?
6. What were the primary problems encountered?
7. Who planned the change?
8. What training did they have?
9. What outside resources were needed?
10. How did they communicate the plan to the rest of the organization during the planning phase?
11. What are the on-going problems?

B. Job Roles and Responsibilities
1. What is the role of the foreman and team leader?
2. How are hourly people involved?
3. What is the role of the committeeman—does he or she have another job? On the team?
4. What is role of the shop committee in the improvement process?
5. What are team responsibilities? (for different kinds of teams?)
6. Staff support—how is it structured?
7. Were any management levels eliminated by the changes?
8. Who is responsible for quality?
9. Skilled trades use—do they have lines of demarcation? Do they have ''jack of all trades''?

C. General Questions about the Union
1. What is the involvement of the International?
2. Is there a standing union/management committee?
3. Is the union more involved in running the business?
4. How does the union feel about increases in productivity?
5. How does the union view increased technology?
6. What is the degree of rapport between union and management at different levels? (communication/ involvement/information/discussion)
7. Is the union involved in the training program for employees?

D. Changes in the Bargaining Agreement
1. What are the pay classifications?
2. How is overtime decided? How is the contract written?
3. Do they have shop rules? What are they? How do they differ from ours?
4. What types of disciplinary actions are in the shop rules?

E. Measures of Effectiveness—People
1. Absenteeism decline?
2. Turnover reduction?
3. Are clerical employees involved?
4. Housekeeping/safety/health—how are they achieved? Who is responsible?
5. What is the grievance rate?

F. Measures of Effectiveness—Other
1. Good or bad quality—how is it achieved?
2. Cost impact—innovative vs. traditional plant (labor, machines, burden, material).
3. Volume output—productivity—how is it measured? Is the innovative system more productive than the traditional?
4. Skilled trades use—what is the mix?
5. How effective are you in scrap, inventory turnover, and eliminating obsolete materials?
6. Do you have preventive maintenance?

G. Information and Communication System
1. What kind of information? e.g., cost, quality, productivity, other—how do they use it? Who gets it?
2. Performance feedback to teams—what, how often, when, from whom?
3. Is there information sharing about quality?
4. What training has been done?
5. Are performance measurements meaningful to the workforce?

H. Evaluation and Reward System
1. How is performance evaluated?
2. What is rewarded and how?
3. Is there any gain sharing?

4. Is there pay by knowledge? Suggestion programs?
Other incentives for learning and improving?

The team facilitator then arranged the tours to provide ample on-site visiting time for observation, questions and discussions with the hostworkers about the pros, cons, successes and failures of innovative systems and processes, and what, based on experience, **might** have been done differently.

In a de-briefing session following each visit, the team examined the strengths and weaknesses of what it had experienced first-hand. This led in turn to a comprehensive evaluation once the team had returned to home base—with the overall conclusions we've outlined below:

Leadership

. . . In successful approaches first-line managers or supervisors were either carefully selected for or fully trained in the skills required to facilitate implementation. They understood and supported the overall change process.

. . . In unsuccessful approaches first-line managers or supervisors were unprepared to assume their roles, lacked an in-depth understanding of the approach and/or did not support the change process.

Worker participation

. . . In successful approaches the union and hourly employees were involved in developing the approach from its inception and actively supported implementation.

. . . In unsuccessful approaches the plan was developed by management and then ''sold'' to the union and hourly employees.

Training

. . . In successful approaches appropriate training was given to all members of the organization.

. . . In unsuccessful approaches training was inadequate, due either to budget cuts or to poor planning.

Strength and balance

. . . In successful approaches the change process was part of an identifiable central strategy and consisted of many mutually supportive activities aimed at improving quality, productivity, and the quality of worklife.

. . . In unsuccessful approaches, programs were fragmented, implemented by various groups, and lacked a central strategy.

Timing

. . . The most successful approaches were implemented over time rather than in an all-at-once or all-or-nothing-at-all fashion.

. . . The less successful approaches were implemented as a totality. This abrupt shift invariably caused fear, frustration, and misunderstanding among the workforce.

Consistency at the top

. . . Successful organizations were almost invariably characterized by a top management and union leadership that projected an image consistent with the approach being implemented.

. . . Leaders of less successful plants failed to project an image consistent with their intended approaches, either through a misunderstanding of their role or because they lacked the insight or skills to project such an image.

Incentives and rewards

. . . Organizations that made rapid improvement provided their workforce with a way to share in the financial gain stemming from increased learning, involvement, quality and/or productivity. Also, provisions were made to assure timely and ample non-financial recognition and feedback to individuals and groups.

. . . In approaches that took longer to show results, improvement was acknowledged only through haphazard and vague compliments given to large groups of employees.

Performance Measurement

. . . In successful organizations performance levels were known by everyone based on measures everyone understood. Almost every aspect of organizational performance was measured and improvement in these measures was a commonly accepted goal.

. . . In unsuccessful organizations measurements were lacking. Comments such as "It's too early to tell if the process is working" were typical. Employees were unsure of how the plant was performing and did not comfortably accept a part in improving performance.

Organizational philosophy

. . . In successful approaches the improvement plan grew organically from a clear overall statement of philosophy or mission.

. . . In less successful approaches the organization had no guiding philosophy.

The plant tours had taught the Livonia Planning Team a set of invaluable lessons immediately clear to its members. They had identified the elements common to the most successful applications of structural and procedural change. They had isolated the stumbling blocks. They recognized that, given the right ingredients, they themselves could succeed as others had succeeded. They saw the clear reality of a workable operating philosophy and plan for Livonia, combining the best of what they had experienced with their own innovative systems, structured to create a comprehensive, integrated approach.

The tours also put the final touches on the team building process. Traveling together provided the informal contact necessary for development of a true team spirit among the team members.

In the days to come the Livonia Planning Team would in fact use every lesson it had learned, incorporated into a dynamic process of transformation. It was now prepared to shape the first symbol of that process: a concise written statement of philosophy.

REVIEW/GUIDELINES/APPLICATION

TRANSFORMATION: STAGE 5

Managing A Team Development Process

Following its orientation the Planning Team undergoes a comprehensive program designed to align the group and develop them into an effective working body that is cohesive, mutually supportive, knowledgeable, responsible, perceptive, and efficient. The formulation and administration of this team development program is the responsibility of the team facilitator acting alone or in collaboration with a highly trained outside consultant.

The program is in three phases:

Phase One: Basic Skills

(a) Instruction in rational approaches to **problem solving and decision making** gives the Planning Team the tools for clear thinking and productive action. It gives the team a systematized way to appraise situations, analyze decisions and problems, and avoid possible negative future consequences of actions taken in the present.

(b) Training in the **principles of human behavior** gives the Planning Team the insight it will need to solve problems and design systems and operations that will work not in the abstract but in the real world. This is only possible by understanding people's needs, attitudes, motivation, expectations, and how they respond and communicate.

(c) In order to design, sell, and implement its important plan, the team must understand and be prepared to overcome **organizational resistance** to the changes it will ask for. It must realize that any change from the status quo may be perceived by others as a threat (on various levels) or as a genuine source of anxiety and fear.

Phase Two: Team Building

Experiences in this part of the development program are designed to build team comfort and confidence, to bond team members more closely together, and to help the group reach a consensus on how it will go about its task.

As a result of team building, the Planning Team will be more communicative, more receptive to feedback, more aware of its strength as a unified decision-making body and better prepared to determine how it will operate.

Phase Three: Enlightenment

This phase exposes the team members to approaches to change previously unknown to them. Working from a base of comprehensive knowledge of the workings of its own organization, the Planning Team is better prepared to evaluate innovative approaches to change found in other organizations.

As a result the team can avoid misjudgments, sift out what is unworkable, identify elements common to successful approaches to change, and formulate a foundation for its own integrated program.

This important stage of positive identifications and consolidation prepares the Planning Team for its first major action: the creation of a statement of its own organization's overall philosophy.

Very few organizations have the internal resources necessary to train and develop a Planning Team. Outside resources should be used where necessary. It is important, however, that someone **within** the organization work closely with outside consultants so that the organization will have an individual to turn to after consulting relationships have ended. Your organization should select consulting groups who are willing to train internal resources to teach their particular technology to the entire workforce.

Many organizations have cut short the development process for a Planning Team, establishing instead union and management quality-of-worklife steering committees and any number of smaller Planning Groups that report to the steering committee. Generally these committees sink under their own weight and become frustrated due to a lack of progress. Additionally these committees sponsor various fragmented activities that never come together into a central change process necessary to generate significant results.

To avoid frustration and failure, a Planning Team should only be activated when there are overall objectives to be met within a given amount of time. Union and management leadership must bestow on the Planning Team both the autonomy and the training to explore comprehensive and integrated changes in the workplace process.

A Model for Team Development

THE JOHARI WINDOW

The importance of self-disclosure and feedback in building interpersonal relationships is illustrated in the Johari Window, named after developers Joseph Luft and Harry Ingram and used to represent the degree of self-awareness and awareness that others have of you in interpersonal relationships.

The window consists of four panes that vary in how much information is available to you and others. The upper-left pane is free information known to you and to others. The upper-right pane is information that you are blind to, but that is available to others. The lower-left pane is information that is known to you but that you hide from others. The lower-right pane is information that is unknown to you and to others.

Self-disclosure increases the amount of information that is known to other people and thus moves the horizontal slat of the window downward as a relationship grows in intimacy. At the same time, the use of feedback from other people can help you to reduce the blind and the unknown areas. At the beginning of a relationship the free area is small in comparison to the other panes of the window (top of figure) whereas in an intimate and trusting relationship the free area has expanded and the hidden, blind and unknown are reduced in size (bottom of figure).[12]

The larger the free area becomes, the more effectively the group performs.

Areas of the Self at the Beginning of a Relationship

	Known to Self	Not Known to Self
Known to Others	Area of Free Activity (Public Self)	Blind Area
Not Known to Others	Avoided or Hidden Area (Private Self)	Unknown Self

Areas of the Self after the Development of a Close Relationship

	Known to Self	Not Known to Self
Known to Others	Area of Free Activity (Public Self)	Blind Area
Not Known to Others	Avoided or Hidden Area (Private Self)	Unknown Self

Chapter 7

Creating A Statement of Operating Philosophy

Just as all laws in the United States must be constitutional—that is, measured against our nation's written statement of guiding moral and ethical principles—all systems and procedures established by an organization should be similarly consistent with *its* written statement of purpose, mission or overall philosophy. This document—one's "industrial constitution," in spirit and intent—is thus both an expression of beliefs, conduct, and commitment and a framework or guide against which all subsequent actions and changes can be evaluated. Here is what William Ouchi says in *Theory Z:*

> The bedrock of any Z company is its philosophy. The thought of mixing practical business matters with pie-in-the-sky concerns may seem strange, but popular belief aside, philosophy and business are the most compatible of bedfellows. To the extent that practical no-nonsense business decisions come from a consistent, integrated set of ideals, they are more likely to prove successful in the long run. A philosophy can help an organization to maintain its sense of uniqueness by stating explicitly what is and isn't important. It also offers efficiency in planning and coordination between people who share in this common culture. But more than a vague notion of company right-and-wrong,

60

there needs to be a carefully thought-out philosophy, preferably one available to all employees in booklet form.[13]

The statements reproduced below illustrate the general form and language of typical expressions of overall organizational philosophy. Since neither purports to be an operating *plan*, the generalizations are of course intentional: "to promote the general welfare" . . . "harmony and cooperation" . . . "built on a foundation of trust" . . . "offered an opportunity to participate," and so on—all, broad-based foundations for present and future action.

PACKARD ELECTRIC - WARREN BRANCH OPERATIONS

Operating Philosophy

WE BELIEVE . . .

Every business has a responsibility to its customers, its employees, and the community in which it exists and shall strive to satisfy the needs and security of each.

We share in the belief that a successful business provides and maintains an environment for change and is built on a foundation of trust, where every person is treated with respect and offered an opportunity to participate. We are totally committed to the patience, dedication and cooperation necessary to build this foundation.

We also believe that this can be accomplished through a functioning partnership built on the wisdom, the knowledge and the understanding of the employees, the union and management.

MATSUSHITA ELECTRIC COMPANY

BASIC BUSINESS PRINCIPLES

To recognize our responsibilities as industrialists, to foster progress, to promote the general welfare of society, and to devote ourselves to the future development of world culture.

EMPLOYEES CREED

Progress and development can be realized only through the combined effort and cooperation of each member of our company. Each of us, therefore, shall keep this idea constantly in mind as we devote ourselves to the continuous improvement of our company.

THE SEVEN SPIRITUAL "VALUES"

- National Service Through Industry
- Fairness
- Harmony and Cooperation
- Struggle for Betterment
- Courtesy and Humility
- Adjustment and Assimilation
- Gratitude

To develop its statement the fifteen-member Planning Team split into three equal groups, with each working out its own version of the text. The best elements of each were then combined to create one comprehensive and mutually acceptable statement. It is important to stress that this refinement process ended only when every member agreed with every point included in the finished document. Alignment of the Planning Team is complete when this once diverse group adopts a noble purpose—and every individual commits himself or herself to achieving that purpose. This team is now ready to begin the design of an organization in which all employees and groups will align themselves with the overall operating philosophy.

The Livonia Engine Plant Operating Philosophy was then shared with the top management group and labor union leaders, approved, handsomely reproduced (in calligraphy on parchment), signed, attractively framed and prominently displayed throughout the organization.

Why the deluxe treatment? Because in so treasuring our new-born "constitution," everyone who shared in its creation was expressing in concrete form his or her agreement with, respect for and full commitment to both its ideals and the transformation that this philosophy would generate.

The lessons learned by the Planning Team—specifically, the conclusions it drew at the close of its enlightenment phase of training—are clearly at the root of this text, reproduced below in full. The all-important aspects of skilled guidance, worker participation, comprehensive training, appropriate timing, incentives and rewards, and leadership consistency and commitment are either spelled out or implied throughout the document.

LIVONIA ENGINE PLANT

Operating Philosophy

A changing business environment requires that:

TOGETHER through trust, communication and respect for the individual, WE WILL BUILD an organization supportive of all employees in the development and utilization of their knowledge, ability and skill towards the achievement of personal as well as organizational goals.

Inherent in these goals is the production of a high-quality, competitive product in a clean and safe plant, contributing to the success of Cadillac and its employees.

In committing to the above philosophy, we recognize the development of the Livonia plant environment to be a dynamic process. Our success will be dependent upon support from the entire Cadillac organization in the consistent and patient application of this philosophy.

We cannot recall exactly what went through our minds when we completed our Operating Philosophy statement, but we have since developed the feeling that there was some parallel with Winston Churchill's comment: **"Now is not the end. It is not even the beginning of the end. But it is, perhaps, the end of the beginning."**

REVIEW/GUIDELINES/APPLICATION

Creating A Statement of Operating Philosophy

Although the simple document we have described in this chapter amounts to no more than one sheet of paper, its physical size in no way reflects the accomplishment it represents or the implications it contains for the safeguarding of the organization's future.

Should you think otherwise, stop for a moment to ask yourself when, throughout the history of your company, your organization and union leadership has cooperatively. . .

. . . reached a consensus on the need to change?

. . . found a workable means to effect that change?

. . . endorsed a group to scrutinize the entire organization and develop a comprehensive plan?

. . . taken the time and made the effort to select people who would be responsible for planning and implementing that change?

. . . thoroughly prepared those people to understand and successfully accomplish their mission?

. . . agreed in writing with a set of governing principles on which your organization would be modeled?

Sad to say, most of us are likely to answer ''Never.'' And yet not one of these questions should be considered impractical, illogical, unreasonable, or (as all of us have said at one time or another) ''Out of the question.''

Everything we have described to this point can be done elsewhere. It is not the product of our size or resources or line of work. It is the result of a realistic assessment of where we stood, a belief in the value of a change for the better, a genuine desire to translate a dream into reality and a commitment to a day-by-day program designed to reach that goal.

The "Livonia Statement" was to be the first tangible product of its Planning Team—a true milestone for the plant and a visible sign of the team's growth from training to "graduate" activity! Although many organizations produce such statements, most often they are generated by the manager alone and forced on the remainder of the workforce. It is significant that the Livonia philosophy was the product of a Planning Team representing a true cross-section of the organization.

PART THREE

INTRODUCTION

A word about change.

Change is a fragile, vulnerable thing. It is that moment in the life of an organization when the status quo—the comfortable condition of "things as they are"—is about to be swept away, when the security of established patterns is threatened.

Change is not some sort of mechanical abstraction. It involves people—individuals with dreams, expectations, fixed attitudes, all degrees of motivation, ways of thinking and behaving. Without the sympathetic participation of these imperfect, vulnerable human beings—which is to say, **all** of us—change has no meaning or substance.

Because the transformation that so concerns us is a **continual process of dynamic evolution**, in no way can those who would take on the role of leadership for change grasp a sense of the appropriate timing or pace of that change without grasping, simultaneously, a sense of the fears, anxieties and aura of threat that lie on the dark side of those very people who will give the process of change its reality.

Each step in the journey of transformation can be taken **only when the organization has the capacity and capability to fully understand and absorb it.**

It is sheer folly to "shoot for the stars" and raise expectations to unsupportable heights only to have the innovation or revolutionary plan or extraordinary change come crashing back to earth. We cannot imagine a surer way to undermine a program of change, or worse, destroy its credibility in the eyes of its witnesses.

In one plant we visited, management, intent on swift implementation of its improvement program, abruptly removed time clocks for hourly employees—a seemingly simple act that was, however, both unprecedented and poorly timed. The workforce, lacking an ambiance of mutual trust and cooperative spirit, **was simply not ready for it**. As a result abuse and in-fighting developed, and this comparatively insignificant change threatened the entire improvement process!

Another plant implemented a profit-sharing program as part of its "socio- technical" improvement plan. Again, the organization was not ready for it; the plant had not operated long enough to assess even its "normal" productive output. When management realized its error and announced a backdown from its stated "permanent formula," the consequences were practically assured: trust throughout the organization was destroyed and the entire process was prematurely terminated.

It is in such statements from the workforce as "It's too early to see results" or "Well, what can you expect; we've just begun" or "I could've told you it wouldn't work" that we hear the signs of leadership's insensitivity to the individual's innate fears and human concerns.

Knowing all this, what happens when we **do** implement too much or too little change at any given time?

If we grasp from the start that organizational transformation is a dynamic process—that is, a process in continual motion, of constant growth—and if the process is anchored by everyone's belief in its values and by full, unstinting communication among all its participants, then a momentary reversal can be taken in stride as a natural step in that growth rather than as an attacking blow to the system itself.

Chapter 8

From Philosophy to Plan/Step 1

Structure, Expectations, Relationships

Abbott Bicycle Corporation (ABC) was in trouble. Faced with cost increases, labor problems and stiff competition from Japan, Mr. Abbott himself was already suffering chest pains. His head finance officer talked about shutting down within the year; Jack, over in quality control, was mailing out resumes; Local 1234 was cornering him on every issue.

Desperate for a solution, Abbott read every business book he could get his hands on. All were interesting but didn't tell the complete story or explain how to make needed improvements, all that is but one . . . Well, why not!? This idea of cooperatively transforming the workplace was something he'd never thought much about. Too busy running ABC. Too tied in with doing business the way he'd been taught. Nonetheless, after reading this book Abbott had a vision of what his company could become.

None of the key people at ABC had ever talked to the guys at Local 1234 as equal partners facing a tough business situation. No one had ever seriously considered worker participation in running—**actually running!**—ABC. No one in management dared suggest that ABC's structure and systems might have some shortcomings, or that a reevaluation was in order.

In a month's time Abbott had moved quickly. He'd presented this idea—"comprehensive and integrated change," the book had called it—to his managers. He'd called up Charlie over at the Local headquarters and talked to **him** about it. Maybe it was the crisis that did the trick. Maybe everyone had run out of answers. Maybe the people at both ABC and the Local union realized they were both declining organizations and what the next round of layoffs might mean. At any rate everyone was willing to give it a try.

By the end of the next month there had been real progress. Mr. Abbott, Jack and the other managers had sat down with the Local union and actually reached a consensus on the need to change the ABC situation. (It was the first time in anyone's memory that they had agreed on **anything**!) They even agreed that every aspect of the business must be questioned and changed where necessary. Everyone had a unique viewpoint and valuable input. They came up with an ambitious set of overall objectives. From there on in they followed the suggested program pretty faithfully, wrangling a bit over selection of an ABC Planning Team but finally making some good choices. They bit the bullet in setting up funds and in developing a practical schedule for the team. They found an outside consultant who really knew his business of training the team. Then, keeping the faith as best they could, Mr. Abbott and Charlie and all the others waited for developments.

Then the day arrived. There was that beautifully printed document—"The ABC Operating Philosophy"—all signed, sealed, and delivered to the organization! The Planning Team had done a good job: the statement talked about mutual trust, how they would help each other, how they would all pull together to make ABC a success, how the workforce would be treated like **people**, how there must be improvements in quality, productivity and employee development and involvement, and how Mr. Abbott and Charlie and all the others were committed to making all of this work. "Maybe," thought Mr. Abbott and Charlie in unison, "we've finally turned this thing around once and for all." But what was the next step? Where were they supposed to go from there? The suggestion in the book seemed obvious once they had read it!

> Action begins in the most logical way: You must evaluate your current operation: How does it work? How is it run? What are its strengths and weaknesses? What kind of human resources are available?
>
> When we sit down to do the homework of analysis, let's be

wary of the trap under the first step: We tend to gloss over or minimize the **importance** of the systems and relationships that are at the heart of our business.

No matter how slick its surface or well appointed its offices may be, a typical organization is frankly a hodgepodge: a little of this, a pinch of that, a system that barely gets by, another system that's fine, unproductive relationships, good relationships, adversarial relationships, and so on.

When Abbott and all the others stopped to think about it, it was true that they had been locked into their patterns and daily problems; that they had spent years interpreting, adjusting, tinkering, and often subverting ABC's systems and subsystems. Enough tinkering had gone on to the point that the present ABC no longer reflected its intended design or stated purpose. "Faced with this reality of a patchwork quilt of organizational elements," the book went on, "we must find a way to sort through it, to decipher it in order to find out what's **really** going on in your company."

Mr. Abbott's company differs from all other companies in surface only: the product it turns out, the particular services it offers, its size and resources, the actual people who work there, and so on. On the other hand it is **identical** to all other companies in a most fundamental way: **It has a structure**, or, to be more precise, **three** structures that are intricately interlocked. It is only by understanding this trio, how each part works, and how all three work together that ABC's Planning Team (or yours, or ours) can possibly visualize a **more** effective organization. To build the new, we must start with a working knowledge of what we already have in our hands.[14]

STRUCTURE

The formal structure: This is the easiest to analyze: It is your organization chart and written job descriptions. Working with this data the Planning Team must now address these questions:

1. Is this current data? Should it be reviewed before you go on?

2. Is the formal structure doing the job it was designed to do?

3. What are its strengths? its weaknesses and problems? its bottlenecks?

4. Is the formal structure "fat" (overdone, complex) or "lean" (tight, economically direct)?

5. How is information passed through the points of the chart? Are these reporting relationships clear to all concerned? Does this setup facilitate or impede the flow of information?

6. Does the formal structure facilitate problem solving by providing effective connections among affected personnel?

7. Does the formal structure support cooperative teamwork? Or does it foster destructive competition or adversarial confrontation?

8. How and to what degree are the various functions separated?

9. Which functions within the structure have expanded beyond their original design? Did this happen to meet organizational needs? for political reasons? to satisfy egos?

10. What might be gained by changing this structure?

11. In the event of restructuring, where might you expect to find the greatest resistance to change?

12. In what way is the formal structure consistent or inconsistent with the company's overall operating philosophy?

    The value of an analysis of this sort lies in its efficiency in helping us cut down to the bare bones of the formal structure. It forces us to take nothing for granted—neither outmoded jobs, nor self-justifying additions and changes, nor a self-perpetuating system, nor the absence of available alternatives, nor "politics as usual."

The informal structure: Define this as "how things **really** get done." An analysis of this structure is especially provocative because of its bearing on the validity of the company's **formal** structure: The degree to which we depend on the informal structure to do the job says a great deal about the true worth and appropriateness of the organization chart, the job descriptions, and the policies and practices associated with both. There is now a new set of questions to be answered:

1. How does the company implement improvements in the quality of its products or services?

2. How does the company implement decisions affecting production and efficiency?

3. How does the company implement decisions affecting personnel policy?

4. How does the company implement financial decisions?

5. Which individual(s) or group(s) can singlehandedly determine whether or not a decision is effectively carried out?

6. Can you identify any influential groups whose operations **are already consistent** with the company's new overall philosophy?

7. Can you identify any influential groups whose operations **have now become inconsistent** with the new overall philosophy?

The power structure: We are now concerned with the people who make decisions and exert influence not through ''position'' but rather through **personal** power: someone with tight political connections . . . another with exceptional skills . . . someone who knows the organization inside-out, and so on.

All of us know people whose powers hardly match their positions: a vice president of personnel with veto power over product selections and marketing promotions; a retired union president whose opinion, even **in absentia**, could make or break management-union cooperation; the list is long indeed.

An accurate reading of the current power structure helps the Planning Team identify where in the organization it may have to turn for support of its improvement plan or, on the other hand, how it must handle a realignment affecting those in power:

1. Who within the managerial ranks has the power to implement change?

2. Who in the union has the power to approve and implement change?

3. Who are the influential leaders in the workforce?

4. Who in the organization is the first to have critical information?

5. Which person in the power structure is likely to support a new operating plan? Who will oppose it? Whose power base will be threatened?

6. If the new operating plan runs counter to the current power structure, what can be done to change, neutralize, or remove those in opposition?

7. Whose power is used in a manner that **is already consistent** with the new operating philosophy?

8. Whose power is used in a manner that **has now become inconsistent** with the new operating philosophy?

Once the Planning Team has analyzed the organization's current formal, informal and power structures, it will be ready to identify specific areas that appear to be either in synchronization with or in opposition to the new overall operating philosophy. This is an important preparatory step in the process of structural redesign, pointing to elements that should be retained, changed, minimized, or eliminated.

Expectations

The future success of the Abbott Bicycle Corporation will depend not only on a structure consistent with its philosophy; **it will also hinge on the philosophical consistency of a network of expectations**. Why should this concern Mr. Abbott and the ABC Planning Team? What do "expectations" have to do with ABC's efforts to pull its declining fortunes out of the fire?

The level and type of expectations that surround ABC's total operation are excellent indicators of the company's effectiveness. Does Mr. Abbott expect a good year? (We already know the answer to that one!) Does ABC marketing expect a strong, mediocre, or weak response to its campaigns? Does ABC production expect to turn out a top-quality bicycle? Do the workers expect steady work with good pay? Do Mr. Abbott's customers expect a well made product? Are these expectations consistent **within** each group inside and outside the Abbott Bicycle Corporation? Are these expectations consistent or inconsistent with ABC's new operating philosophy?

The importance of this analysis lies in its identification of appropriate expectations that are properly communicated, consistent and mutually supportive. Which ones already exist? Which ones should be present in the "ideal" ABC of tomorrow?

In the following questions the word "group" should be applied, in turn, to (a) corporate management, (b) operational management, (c) the labor union, (d) the workforce and (e) the customers.

1. What is the group's top priority?

2. What are the group's expectations concerning productivity and product quality?

3. What other performance expectations does this group have?

4. Despite its expectations about productivity, product quality, performance, and so on, what will **satisfy** this group?

5. What do the members of this group really expect **for themselves** from the current organization?

6. Compare the expectations of this group to those of other groups. Are they in harmony? in conflict?

7. Are any or all of these expectations clearly communicated to others? vaguely communicated? hidden entirely?

8. Can you identify the expectations that are either **already consistent** or that have now **become consistent** with the new operating philosophy?

The **existence** of a given expectation should not be confused with its **appropriateness** in the transformed organization. While some will certainly be sufficiently high to challenge the new organization, others may be too insignificant or unrealistic for serious consideration. That is an assessment that the Planning Team must make as it develops and implements its operating plan.

Relationships

Assuming that it has done a good job so far—the Planning Team has now evaluated the structures and surrounding expectations of Mr. Abbott's troubled company—the ABC Planning Team should have a fairly easy time with the last area to be examined: the relationships within the organization, how they work, and why they break down.

This analysis is done by answering the question, "**How do members of the following groups work and interrelate?**"

(a) within management alone
(b) within the labor union alone
(c) within the workforce alone
(d) between management and the union
(e) between management and the workforce
(f) between the union and the workforce

and then by answering the questions that have involved bottom-line issues from the start of this whole examination:

How does each relationship (a-f above) **affect the total organization?**

Is each relationship (a-f above) **consistent or inconsistent with the new operating philosophy?**

In our experience at Livonia, **the best possible relationship**—within each group, between any two, among all three, and of any and all to the **total** organization—is the inevitable product of this blend: a network of mutually supportive relationships; openly communicated expectations; the full support of a rational structure; and a consistency among all these elements with the organization's operating philosophy.

Properly analyzed, all of these ingredients—structure, expectations, and relationships—form the basis for the most effective game plan for Mr. Abbott's Planning Team (and yours, and ours). It now has a clear set of guidelines to help in the design of an improvement plan. It understands the strengths on which it can build. It understands the weak and critical areas. It has identified points of consistency and conflict. It is more in touch with the amount of time and degree of planning necessary to effect major changes. It can better assess the willingness, throughout the organization, to change structures, alter historic roles, and change expectations and their measurement.

The hard homework done, the Planning Team can now afford to dream a bit as they answer the provocative question (in Chapter 10),

"Where do we want to be?"

REVIEW/GUIDELINES/APPLICATION

TRANSFORMATION: STAGE 7

The "Tough" Homework: Analyzing the Present Organization

If it seems that the Planning Team has cruised smoothly up to and past its first task (the written statement of operating philosophy), then it must now downshift to first gear to handle the first comprehensive analyses of the present organization. This is a slow and careful hill climb, full of twists and turns.

The starting place is the team's realization that the company, if it is like most, may be a hodgepodge of systems, operations, and relationships. Years of adjusting this element and that, just to get by from day to day, from quarter to quarter, may have gradually and imperceptibly downgraded or badly eroded the company's working parts. The Planning Team must consequently understand what is going on **now** if it is to come up with a sensible, realistic operating plan for the company's future. It must find out how the organization works, how it is run, what its strengths and weaknesses are, and the kind of human resources that are available to it.

This is indeed tough homework. To have any positive impact at all on the transformation process, the analyses must be scrupulously honest and precise. They cannot gloss over what is obvious, and they must not be compromised by vested interests or personal relationships.

The Planning Team's first job is to analyze the formal, informal, and power structures of the organization.

Analysis of the **formal structures** is based on data derived from the company's organization chart and job descriptions. It focuses on what does and does not work, on the efficiency of reporting relationships and the flow of information, on the validity of current functions and on the influence of the formal structure on the working ambiance of the company. At the same time it tries to isolate areas that are potentially supportive of or resistant to change.

Analysis of the **informal structure** is based on a frank appraisal of how things **really** get done in the company. Sometimes this is in alignment with the formal structure, but it frequently operates independently and in spite of surface formalities. This analysis focuses on **actual** implementation procedures: for quality improvement; for decisions affecting productivity, efficiency, personnel policy, finances, and so on; and for follow-through assessments of previous decisions and actions. It also tries to identify influential groups whose operations are consistent or inconsistent with the new operating philosophy.

Analysis of the **power structure** is based on an identification of those whose positions may not match their strong influence on company policies and decisions. It focuses on influential people in the managerial ranks, in the union and in the workforce; on those who may or may not support a new operating plan; and on those whose use of power is consistent or inconsistent with the new operating philosophy.

The Planning Team must next analyze the network of **expectations** that surrounds the organization's total operations. These strong indicators of the company's effectiveness exist both inside and outside of the organization: in corporate and operational management, in the labor union, and among the workforce and the company's customers.

Paying attention to each in turn, the team assesses that group's priorities and both its expectations about and level of satisfaction with product quality, productivity and the quality of worklife. The team must also determine how well these expectations are communicated, and whether or not they are consistent from group to group and fundamentally consistent with the new operating philosophy itself.

The last analysis of the organization deals with **relationships** within management, the union, and the workforce, between each of these groups and the other and between each group and the total organization. As always the Planning Team must assess these elements for their consistency with the company's operating philosophy.

We cannot overstate the powerful influence of all of these analyses on the development of the organization's operating plan. An assessment that falls short of impartiality, that is imprecise, that avoids key issues, or that is simply too shallow for its purpose will only serve to undermine the value of the transformation process and the stability of the plan itself.

Strengths and weaknesses exist in all organizations. They must be recognized and dealt with fairly and fearlessly. On the other hand we can also choose to continue to "tread lightly" . . . **but with what consequences**?

Chapter 9

From Philosophy to Plan/Step 2

"Best Organization:" The World of Should

Over the years we have all been part of a number of organizations. Think about the schools you have attended, perhaps a church group or a community chorus, a club or fraternal organization, even an informal sports team or a place where you work out once or twice a week. You have an opinion about these groups: a good feeling? a fond memory? a criticism? some thoughts about how things were run?

Which is the one club or social organization or work organization that you like best?	_____
Why did you choose that one? (List one or two reasons.)	1. . . . . 2. . . . .

How do you rate. . .

	Excellent	Good	Fair	Poor
(a) the way it is organized?	____	____	____	____

(b) the way it is run?   —   —   —   —

(c) the relationship among its
     members?   —   —   —   —

(d) the level of expectations
     that the organization
     generates among its
     members?   —   —   —   —

(e) the quality of its activities?   —   —   —   —

(f) the results of its activities?   —   —   —   —

When the Livonia Planning Team members compared and categorized their answers to this informal quiz (called "Best Organization"), the results were a revelation: Their reasons for selecting the various organizations they listed were almost a direct translation of the descriptions in their own statement of overall operating philosophy! The team could not have had a more down-to-earth validation of the rightness of its document, nor a more timely reminder that the ideal structuring of an ideal organization must be founded on the most basic humanistic principles and beliefs.

"Best Organization" was the beginning of a new stage of work for the team. Using all of the information it had gathered to date, the group was now asked to replace analysis with creative thinking and imaginative projection, to focus not on what the organization had been or was that day but on what it should be. As a follow-up to the homework on organizational analysis, this free-wheeling give-and-take was a welcomed change of pace . . . and a step closer to the formation of an overall operating plan.

The "script" of the two-day process went something like this:

FACILITATOR:

"I would like each one of you to describe what our organization would look like in five years if all the needed changes were made, the correct decisions arrived at and the statement of overall philosophy wholly adopted by the entire organization.

"To get the answers we need we've got to shift mental gears away from analysis and, in fact, totally **reverse** our customary thinking. Where analysis begins with structure and ends with relationships, our new creative work asks us to do just the opposite: It's impossible to define a desired structure—that's our new goal—without first identifying the desired relationships within that structure.

"In short, we have to develop a structure to support relationships as we visualize them and to support the purpose of the organization as we understand it.

"Now I'd like each one of you to think about this question: **Can you describe the ideal relationships you would like to find in our future organization?**

"Remember that we're talking about a complex network that includes management, the union and the workforce. There are relationships within each group, relationships **between** groups and relationships between each group and the total organization.

"Let's hear from each one of you in turn, Harry . . .?"

PLANNING TEAM:

Each person shares his or her views. The entire team then works to reach a consensus on the various relationships that **should** exist within and among the organization's groups. Throughout this process the facilitator keeps track of the descriptions on a large easel pad; the members keep notes as they go.

A few examples of the relationships discussed by the Livonia Planning Team are:

- *Role of Supervisor*: Supervisors should assist workers to perform—not police the workforce.

- *Worker and Management*: Treat all employees equally with no second class citizens.

- *Role of the Committeeman*: Committeemen should be involved with management in the day-to-day operation of the plant.

- *Quality Control*: Stop finger pointing between the quality department and manufacturing and work together to solve quality problems.

- *Union and Management*: Cooperative problem- solving approach to solve minor problems on a daily basis.

- *Skilled Trades*: Develop systems to make skilled trades feel a part of the overall production effort.

FACILITATOR:

"OK. Now let's move on to the next step. When you analyzed **expectations**, you took a long, hard look at past and present conditions. But now we're looking into the future: We want to project the kinds of expectations that would be ideal five years down the line.

"We'll consider six questions, applying each one in turn to our customers, the corporate management, the operational management, the union, and the workforce.

"Let's move around the table starting with Margie. Here's the first question . . .

The facilitator aims for total input, once again keeping track of the responses on the easel pad.

1. "What should be the group's top priority?

2. What should be the group's expectations concerning productivity, product quality, and employee involvement and development?

3. What other performance expectations should this group have?

4. What should the members of this group expect for themselves from the organization?

5. How should the expectations of this group compare to those of the other group(s)?

6. How should these expectations be communicated to the other group(s) and to the total organization?"

PLANNING TEAM:

Once again each person shares his or her views, and the team works toward a consensus on the kinds of expectations that each group should have in the ideal organization of the future.

A few examples of the expectations discussed by the Livonia Planning Team are:

- *Cost*: Produce all products at a cost that is competitive.

- *Housekeeping*: Have a clean and safe plant.

- *Training*: Help all employees with skills needed to perform well in the new organization.

- *Performance Feedback*: Individuals and groups should get information about performance which is meaningful.

- *Reward System*: Reward the right things.

- *Product Quality*: Number one in the corporation and improve dramatically with respect to warranty and customer complaints.

FACILITATOR:

"You've agreed on the expectations you think most desirable, but we must make sure that they meet the following conditions:

(a) The expectations should be uniform across all groups in the organization.

(b) The expectations should be mutually supportive, consistent, and harmonious among all groups.

(c) The expectations should be consistent with and supportive of the new overall philosophy.

(d) The expectations should be realistic, yet high enough to challenge the organization.

(e) The expectations should be open to clear communication throughout the organization."

PLANNING TEAM:

The team now verifies that a given expectation meets all of these conditions. If it does not, it must be adjusted to bring it into line with these standards.

FACILITATOR:

"By defining the relationships and expectations you'd like to find in our future organization, you've established a foundation for its structure.

"But now you're in a position to cut away the flab of informal structure and power structure: As we've seen, these are **excesses** that evolve when the formal structure doesn't do the job it's been designed to do! That's when the informal structure develops to accomplish a given task and the power structure begins to sink independent roots. That's exactly what we want to avoid.''

PLANNING TEAM:

Several team members ask for a review of the makeup of the formal structure and a brief rundown of points they should consider.

FACILITATOR:

''Most people think of an organization's formal structure as a sort of family tree, with the boss in the top spot and the branches spreading downward as the various levels of responsibility open outward.

''However, for our purposes we want to reverse the perspective **by first structuring what's going on down there on the plant floor**. If we're going to transform the organization we can't afford to follow the old conventions: It's precisely that traditional way of thinking that has triggered this whole process of change.

''So we must start with **Work Groups**, which are in effect the basic 'building blocks'' at the foundation of the organization.

''Then, moving upward, we need **Support Groups** and **Support Systems** . . and, at the top of the structure, the **First Level of Management** and **Higher Levels of Management** all operating in a consistent manner.

''Once we've labeled these five parts of the formal structure, we've got to describe their **relationships** in sufficient detail to explain and clarify the following areas:

    (a) levels and positions

    (b) the various functions of these five parts

    (c) responsibilities

    (d) reporting relationships

    (e) how we expect information to flow throughout the formal structure.''

PLANNING TEAM:

The team has its work cut out for it as it is now faced with articulating **exactly** what the organization of the future would look like. All of the "should be's" of relationships and expectations come into play as the team builds a solid, effective, and workable formal structure from the ground up.

A few examples of the objectives for a formal structure discussed by the Livonia Planning Team are:

- *Top Management Group*: Top management should be a team and more concerned with the overall plant than their own area.

- *Job Classifications*: Don't draw too many boxes around people as flexibility helps teamwork.

- *Skilled Trades*: Establish a system to more effectively use skilled trades and to develop the skills needed in the future.

- *Material Handling*: Build the material people into the overall manufacturing effort.

- *Job Responsibilities*: Define responsibilities in terms of team responsibilities not individuals.

- *Basic Building Block*: Go with a team concept on the work floor and allow people to work together as if they had their own business.

FACILITATOR:

"You've worked hard to outline a formal structure for our organization, but now we've got to check it out to assure ourselves that it's really what it should be! Let's take a slow and careful look at **everything** to see how each element stands up to each of these questions:

1. Does it take advantage of the strengths **that already exist** in the current organizational structure?

2. Are the reporting relationships clear?

3. Is the flow of information appropriate?

4. Will the separation of functions promote teamwork among the various groups? At the same time does it avoid foreseeable conflict?

5. Is the formal structure "lean," that is, economically direct and uncluttered?

6. In reviewing the **general** direction of our new overall operating philosophy, is the formal structure consistent with its aims?

"There's one question left to answer . . . and it's a crucial one. Before I ask it, let me quote this passage from our statement of philosophy:

"We will build an organization supportive of all employees in the development and use of their knowledge, ability and skill towards the achievement of personal as well as organizational goals.

"From the beginning of our work, we've all realized that this special regard for the Work Group is imperative if we are to have any realistic hope of turning this whole organization around. Obviously our traditional 'business-as-usual' attitude has been a major source of trouble when the potential of human resources is ignored.

"Let's think hard about his one. Here's the last question . . .

7. Is our new concept of the Work Group—our basic 'building block' — consistent with our philosophy?"

PLANNING TEAM:

The team has done its homework, as the results of this questioning prove. Almost without exception (an item here and there needs refinement), the members have remained well aware of the strengths and weaknesses of the current organization and have kept a clear mental picture of what **is** and of what **should be**.

For a final check-and-balance, they place their outline side by side with a description of the current organization. The implications are clear enough: **The Planning Team must now develop an overall operating plan that effectively and in logical stages bridges the gulf between the old and the new.**

REVIEW/GUIDELINES/APPLICATION

TRANSFORMATION: STAGE 8

A Creative Process: Visualizing the Organization of the Future

In its second step from an operating philosophy to an operating plan, the Planning Team leaves organizational analysis behind, embarking on an imaginative projection of what the organization of the future **should** be. Each team member is asked to describe how, in his or her opinion, the organization would look in five years if three conditions would have been met by that time:

(a) All needed changes have been made.

(b) All correct decisions have been made.

(c) The statement of overall philosophy has been wholly adopted by the entire organization.

Reversing the analytic sequence of structure—relationships—expectations, this free exchange of ideas focuses on visualized relationships and expectations **in preparation for** a concluding definition of the future organization's formal structure.

The Planning Team considers relationships within management, the union and the workforce; those between any two groups; and those between each group and the total organization.

The Team must also consider the expectations of the organization's customers, its corporate and operational management, the union and the workforce.

When the Planning Team has reached a consensus, it must verify that all projections meet a set of ideal conditions consistent with the new overall operating philosophy.

This articulation of visualized relationships and expectations establishes a foundation for a balanced, effective and efficient formal structure of the future. If the formal structure does the job it is intended to do, neither an informal structure nor a power structure will evolve to take up slack, overcome inefficiency, or supersede formal functions and responsibilities.

The skeleton of a formal structure consists of Work Groups, Support Groups, Support Systems, a First Level of Management and Higher Levels or Level of Management. Considering the makeup and desired interaction of these five groups, the Planning Team must now describe their relationships in detail, focusing on levels, positions, functions, responsibilities, reporting relationships and the flow of information.

The bulk of its creative process now completed, the team must now verify **the appropriateness of all projections** to its overall visualization of the total organization of the future. It must examine these projections in terms of strengths, communication, the promotion of teamwork, the links among all elements and the degree of consistency between projections and the principles and beliefs underlying the organization's philosophical statement.

Of prime importance, finally, is the degree of consistency between the new organization's philosophy and its projections for the development of human resources within the organization. If transformation is to become a reality, **attention to the needs, worth and potential of the individual must under no circumstances be compromised**.

As you have probably guessed, the one-sidedness of the pseudo-script in the main text of this chapter hardly represents the vigorous give-and-take of the two-day meeting. Although the team facilitator appears to have the best of it, the Planning Team members were anything but passive! If you also assumed that the way we presented this dialogue is intentional, you are right; this is a point we would like to clarify before going on.

What we accomplished at Livonia was the result of an application of a process. Our team drew its conclusions based on its analysis of and projections for a particular business with specific operations and systems. Since your business and ours are different, with special consideration tied to the uniqueness of each, it is the **process** of transformation rather than its detailed outcome that we have tried to stress from the start. For this reason **how** the Livonia Planning Team responded during these sessions seemed to us far more appropriate and useful than **what** its members said or did at a given moment — although we have included specifics about our team's conclusions. This, we think, is the more effective guideline for your own application of the transformation process.

But now we have reached a turning point, as you will see when you read from Chapter 10 to the end of the book.

The conclusions reached by the Livonia team now become intimately interwoven with the process itself. These concern issues of worker autonomy, increased responsibility throughout the workforce, intensive training of all personnel, an innovative pay system, the elimination of traditional distinctions between salaried and hourly employees and more.

The most powerful and influential conclusion, however, concerns the Livonia Planning Team's unqualified support and promotion of **the team concept as a central and unifying force** throughout the new organization. So urgent and prominent was this ideal, moreover, that it immediately became the recurrent main theme of the evolving operating plan and its orchestration over the months of plan implementation.

None of what we will describe in the following chapters is intended as a **fixed** prescription to heal business ills and wounds; it is neither a formula for success nor a waving of the magic cure-all wand. What is it, then? It is a valuable, workable, practical, and highly effective alternative way of doing business. It is an approach that taps the organization's most potent, yet undervalued and misused, asset: its human resources. It is a detailed map for the troubled organization that genuinely seeks answers, solutions, and resolutions.

How responsive you are to the specifics of our overall operating plan and how appropriate you find its application to your own business environment, operations and systems is not important. Its concern for human values, and for human welfare in general, is however a foundation we must all share. With this foundation in hand, the essential contribution of this book is a proven, rational and well-defined process of allowing your organization to develop a plan for transformation tailored to its own uniqueness and stage of development.

Chapter 10

Centerpiece:
The Team Concept

. . . How will the United States adjust to the changing
world economy?

One option is to refuse to acknowledge that there has
been any fundamental change. We can refrain from any
special policies to respond to growing competition and let
world market forces take their course. This path leads to
predictable results:. . . America would be out-competed in
industry after industry. . . . [a] more likely American response to economic change would be to resist it. . . . [but
then] other countries will do the same. International trade
will slow to a trickle. The world economy will stagnate. . . .

There is another path open to America. Its basic direction
is not mysterious: As the rest of the world progresses, we
must also progress if we are to retain our role of economic
leadership. Accommodating world development without
succumbing to the new competition means that we cannot
continue to rely on high-volume, standardized industries
after other countries have become better suited for them.
Rather, our economic future must be rooted in the only
resource that will remain uniquely American: Americans
themselves. The industries that will sustain the next stage of

America's economic evolution will necessarily be based on a skilled, adaptable, and innovative labor force and on a more flexible, less hierarchial organization of work. . . .

America's place in the evolving world economy will increasingly depend on its workers' skills, vigor, initiative, and capacity for collaboration and adaptation. Our future lies in our human capital.[15]

The Livonia Planning Team's vision of the form and character of the new organization was the result of weeks of analysis, visualization, and thoughtful balancing of the organizational objectives. An inseparable part of that vision was the **team concept**: a central, unifying force that would bind the structure and operations of the new organization as well as allow for the desired employee involvement and development.

While the team concept was not spelled out in the team's philosophical statement, its principles can be read between these lines:

Together through trust, communication and respect for the individual, we will build an organization supportive of all employees in the development and use of their knowledge, ability and skill towards the achievement of personal as well as organizational goals.

Faced with their own growth as an autonomous unit—a mutually supportive decision-making body—the team members could only have felt it right and natural to project that positive self-image onto the larger screen, the broader arena, of the organization as a whole. Thus, over time, as work progressed on bridging the gap between the old and the new organization, the team concept served as the foundation on which the structure was built.

In time, the work group—an organized unit of knowledgeable, responsible, mutually interactive and supportive business people—became the centerpiece of the plan that came to be called ''the Livonia Opportunity.'' For those immersed in the development of this ''opportunity,'' the label conjured up whole sets of interlocked images: of a new, enlightened attitude toward individuals; of encouraged responsibility and renewed motivation; of a more direct, more personalized involvement of the workforce in the total business operation; of a radically improved work environment.

As our focus became sharper, and the need for more accurate labels seemed appropriate, the work group became the ''business team,'' and the Livonia Opportunity became, simply, "the Business Team Approach."

We had no illusions that we were reinventing the wheel. Twenty years before our team did its work, organizational psychologist Rensis Likert wrote in *New Patterns of Management*: "...management will make full use of the potential capacities of its human resources only when each person in an organization is a member of one or more effectively functioning work groups that have a high degree of group loyalty, effective skills of interaction, and high performance goals."[16]

Through a model of overlapping work groups—a "participative group" type of management system—Likert expanded his theory to include structural changes in the organization. In his *Social Psychology—An Applied Approach*, Dr. Ronald J. Fisher described these organizational changes. [This approach] "combines supportive leadership with democratic team functioning, creating an interlocking hierarchy of organizational families. Likert saw this as the best way to maximize the motivation of individuals, harness the power of the work group, enhance effective communication and democratic decision making and prevent and resolve conflict most productively."[17]

The author goes on to place Likert's work and other pioneering efforts in this perspective:

> The Scanlon Plan [in which all members of the organization have a say in decision making and a share in the profits] and later sociotechnical experiments in Europe, as organization-wide attempts at change, come close to producing **new forms of work organizations** .... These new forms are attempts to improve both the quality of worklife in terms of satisfaction, and the depth of industrial democracy in terms of employee responsibility and power in decision making. In their aspects of reward structure and authority structure, these approaches to organizational change are beginning to approximate alternative forms of organizations that have been around for some time, particularly the cooperatives found in different parts of Europe and North America and the agricultural **kibbutzim** of Israel. These types of organizations provide alternatives to the predominantly bureaucratic structure of most profit-making and public service organizations.[18]

Drawing from its own direct experience and profiting by such historical models, Livonia's Business Team Approach sought to break new ground based on two realities: the pressing needs of the modern American worker and the pressing needs of the organization for which he or she works. Our mandate was not for superficial modification but for a genuine transformation that would address these needs without hesitation, fear, or backsliding.

Our solution—in the form of an overall operating **plan** consistent with our philosophical statement and business team concept—had to possess the essentials that would, to the best of our abilities to foresee and enact them, comprise a fully integrated and truly comprehensive performance system.

REVIEW/GUIDELINES/APPLICATION

TRANSFORMATION: STAGE 9

Business Teams

The decline of product quality and productivity in America is a complex condition that simple remedies, applied rapidly to achieve short-term results, will not correct. Instead we must undertake a logical, step-by-step approach aimed at two simultaneous goals: enlightenment of all members of the organization to the interlocked conditions of industrial survival and competitive challenge, and implementation of a process of workable change for the better, to be understood and embraced by all members of the organization.

Change for the better must be all-encompassing. It must confront the organization's fundamental philosophy, structure, communications, teamwork, environment, work practices, operating systems and relationships and its condition of mutual trust and mutual support.

Business teams created at Livonia focus on the needs of the entire organization. They balance the company's need for bottom-line results and the individual's need for growth, self-respect, and genuine involvement with and participation in that company's future and fortunes. Business teams focus on short-term goals only insofar as they are consistent with long-term growth of the organization and everyone in it.

The strength of the Business Team approach lies in its ability to integrate sound business practices and the untapped potential of human resources. This integration is performed in a logical, systematic, and supportive manner.

This workplace transformation embraces the effective use of modern technology, but focuses primarily on full contributions from every member of the organization. It stresses progress toward perfection in all areas, by all members. This is, after all, a mature workforce, with beliefs, attitudes and customs rooted in its American upbringing. The transformation process is a continuous, dynamic, **participatory** process of evolution, particularly appropriate for workers in today's America.

At the heart of the workplace transformation is a firm belief in and support of the team concept, of democratic team functioning, of participatory decision making. The business team is thus the cornerstone on which the entire organization is constructed.

Digesting all of these elements we came to define the business team concept in this way:

> It is an organization of work into small autonomous work groups, with supporting system changes so integrated as to encourage and reinforce participation, teamwork, understanding, and commitment towards a single goal: the production of high quality products, on time, within budget, in an environment of openness, honesty, development and trust.

That such an approach to the corporation and its workforce can restore and revitalize the spirit of the American worker is self-evident in comments made by Livonia workers after implementation of our plan:

"People like their jobs, and it shows."

(an hourly employee)

"They aren't saying we are going to treat you like a human being. They're **showing** it. This is something I can see for myself."

(an hourly employee elected as a team leader)

"I haven't written a grievance in months. I go to the team meeting and try to resolve the matter without reducing it to writing."

(a union representative)

"We always heard their feelings. Now they're hearing ours. We feel more a part of the company now."

(a skilled tradesman)

"There's a better rapport between the management and the hourly people. There's not so much hiding and concealment of this and that. It's open."

(an hourly employee)

"At one time it was the foreman versus the union rep, and we'd go at each other. Here it's the coordinator and the rep and we sit down and discuss things intelligently to come up with a mutual agreement and understanding of the problems people in the workforce have. It helps."

(a zone committeeman)

The transformation at Livonia is founded on a basic thought that is the theme of this book: given the appropriate systems and environment, American managers, workers and labor unions can work together in a cooperative atmosphere to outperform any other industrial team in the world. **What we create, we can transform.**

Chapter 11

An Exercise in Rationality

The purpose of an overall operating plan is to ensure that our organizational voyage moves along a well-charted path. We want to know where we're going, how we will get there, what obstacles to avoid and which avenues of exploration and growth best meet our needs.

The plan is an exercise in rationality. It must describe how our organizational approach will be structured at the outset. It must state what will be measured. It must establish procedures for setting performance standards for the business group in all measurable areas. It must describe why, when and how future changes will take place. It must describe the training and development required. It must provide a fertile environment for successful transformation within a context of genuine communication, understanding, participation and flexibility.

A good operating plan reconciles the organization's objectives. Reconciliation occurs when each proposed change in an existing system is clearly described, explained in context, and integrated into the whole with a provision of measuring progress consistent with overall goals.

Livonia's objectives were increased productivity, improved product quality and a substantially enhanced quality of worklife. Our operating plan was thus the official document that would spell out the relationships among these three objectives and how they would be achieved simultaneously.

We have said that the operating plan is an exercise in rationality.

Anything short of a cleanly staged, common sense approach to the labyrinth of organizational change practically guarantees despair at best, chaos at worst. How else could one develop a plan that is integrated, comprehensive, consistent, dynamic, and **understandable** to the entire organization?

Its preparatory work had enabled the Livonia Planning Team to identify general areas where change was required. But it is one thing to recognize the need for change, another to follow a logical progression to a viable operating plan. To ease the way, the team followed a three-part process:

- Faced with a mandate for change in a given area, the team developed alternatives by using the proven rational techniques learned during its training in problem solving and decision making.

- With alternatives in hand, the team used a check-and-balance technique to assure consistency with the philosophy and integration of quality, productivity and quality of worklife.

- Finally, the team designed the best timing and modification process to assure a successful outcome for the change in question.

Using rational process (see Chapter 6)

1. The team addresses a broad concern. It asks for clarification. It needs a **Situation Appraisal**. Having identified areas of needed change (between the current and the ideal organizations), the team breaks down areas of needed change into separate issues. Each issue is seen either as an opportunity or as a problem. Situation Appraisal then identifies the rational process needed to address that issue.

2. If the problem is one of human performance ("The night shift isn't working up to par"), the team embarks on a rational process of **Performance Problem Appraisal** to analyze that problem and identify the true cause.

3. If the problem is within a technical or process area ("Too many rejected units"), the team uses **Problem Analysis** to identify the true cause.

4. The proposed solution to either kind of problem now becomes an opportunity.

5. Once all issues are stated as opportunities, the rational process

of **Decision Analysis** is used to arrive at the best balanced alternative for inclusion in the operating plan.

How does all of this work in a common day-to-day issue?

> In its analysis of the then-current Livonia operations, the Planning Team identified a real problem concerning product quality and productivity. The workforce simply didn't know what was expected of it. Everyone was confused; opinions varied widely; no one had hard facts.
>
> Performance Appraisal identified the true cause of the confusion—simple as it may now seem **after** the fact: **There was no specific, written, mutually agreed-upon list of expectations!** Without such a clear agreement it was a matter (in the workforce's thinking) of quality **or** productivity.
>
> The issue, once identified, became an opportunity for improvement.
>
> Once an opportunity was identified, the planning team utilized Decision Analysis to develop the best balanced alternative to take advantage of the opportunity. The first step in Decision Analysis was to state the opportunity in terms of a decision to be made. The statement the team agreed on was "Select a method to communicate expectations to the workforce."
>
> After having agreed on a decision statement, the team listed objectives that should be met by the method of communicating expectations. The objectives developed by the Livonia Team were:
>
> - The method must be understandable.
>
> - The method must be stated in terms of group performance.
>
> - The method must provide meaningful feedback on a group's performance.
>
> - The method must link groups together through common expectations.
>
> - The method must allow the group to appreciate and monitor its own improvement.

The Planning Team eventually selected an alternative consisting of twenty-eight key performance indicators that measured performance in the areas of productivity, quality and quality of worklife. The twenty-eight measures were communicated in terms of total plant performance and the performance of each business team on a weekly basis.

The selection systems designed by the Planning Team to choose key personnel—which were incorporated into the overall plan and used at Livonia—illustrate how concerns are separated, analyzed and how alternatives developed.

On their plant tours the Planning Team learned that the management image must be consistent with the new philosophy, and that first-line supervisors must possess the requisite skills and attitudes to support the change process. The overall concern was that neither the image nor the skills nor the attitudes existed in the current salaried workforce.

Through Performance Analysis the team concluded that attitude and image were concerns that could not necessarily be remedied by training. The opportunity took the form of a new selection system to be used where flexibility existed for choosing candidates.

A Selection Procedure for the Operating Staff

The first selection concern focused on the top management team. Using the Kepner-Tregoe Decision Analysis process (see footnote 11), the Livonia Planning Team established an overall objective and a set of candidate qualifications for members of the operating staff:

Objective:

To delineate those qualifications that assure a common sharing among staff members of skills, abilities, and personal characteristics conducive to the support and maturation of the Business Team concept;

Qualifications:
- a predisposition to participatory management
- decisiveness in situations that call for leadership, specifically when participation by others is unavailable or inappropriate
- strong communication skills, including the ability and willingness to listen

- mastery of, or the capacity to master, rational and logical problem-solving skills

- a thorough understanding of and commitment to the Business Team concept, including the readiness to forego traditional symbols of power and prestige

- the ability to view the organization and its goals in the broadest terms, including an allegiance to the total organization while carrying out responsibilities within an area of specialization

- the capacity and willingness to cooperate fully with one's colleagues, and to familiarize oneself with all of the disciplines represented in the operating staff

- an existing, specialized skill or ability (such as product engineering, organization development and so on), in order that such expertise can be fed into and shared by the organization

With an objective and qualification criteria developed for selection of candidates, an organization must then decide on the easiest method for assessing personnel. This will depend on the size of the company, the size of the candidate pool and the specific needs of the organization.

Flexibility exists when Team Coordinators can be selected from a large candidate pool. The Planning Team concluded that an organization cannot take the risk of underestimating the importance of a stringent selection process. All too often an hourly workforce will readily adopt operating improvements only to be constrained by a manager too reluctant, or too conservative, or inadequately trained, or insufficiently committed to support the new venture. This sort of disruption is far more costly and time-consuming than the cost and time involved in making an appropriate selection at the start.

A Selection Procedure for First-Level Supervisors

The careful selection of a first-level supervisor, the Team Coordinator, is no less important than that of an operating manager. Because Team Coordinators must function in harmony with the Business Team concept—a role entirely different from that of a foreman in a traditional plant structure—their qualifications are somewhat similar to those of the operating staff; however, the objectives for the selection process, developed by the team through Decision Analysis, are more extensive:

Objectives:

- provide an equal opportunity for all who choose to be candidates
- promote a process of voluntary participation
- create a selection process that is easily understood
- create a selection system that can be continued as an ongoing process
- promote the candidacy of personnel from all disciplines
- encourage the involvement of hourly employees, union officials and management in the selection process
- acknowledge seniority—all other conditions being equal
- create a process that is sufficiently explicit to allow candidates to make an informed choice and sufficiently open to allow candidates to change their decision
- provide full documentation of past performance, as available, as an element of candidate evaluation

Qualifications:

- a desire to try new approaches to a given task or mission
- supervisory experience
- the ability and willingness to work in a team environment
- the ability and willingness to plan and organize and to delegate responsibilities to others
- the ability and willingness to confront conflict
- a capacity for communication, both oral and written and to give and receive feedback
- the ability to make a balanced choice in decision-making or problem-solving situations
- a willingness to work off-shifts
- experience in machining, assembly, quality control, material handling, or in the skilled trades, backed by formal

education and a performance appraisal rating of "competent" or better

Because of the extensive objectives and criteria for this selection system, the alternative that best met the objectives and maximized the chance of evaluating the qualifications was a three-stage process.

Stage 1: Pre-Orientation

During a two-hour session all interested supervisors and general supervisors from the entire Cadillac organization were given a broad overview of the Business Team concept. All participants were given a handout listing the qualifications for Team Coordinator applicants and then invited to sign up for consideration by completing an application form.

The application form asked each candidate the reasons for his or her interest in participation and in trying new approaches and a detailed summary of his or her supervisory experience, education, training and specialization.

Out of a supervisory population of 1500 people, over 400 candidates volunteered to continue in the selection process.

Stage 2: Pre-Screening

Pre-screening of candidates was based on the completed application form.

To guarantee fairness, applicants' names were removed and replaced by a numerical code. An evaluation was then carried out by a committee consisting of representatives from quality control, material handling, production, personnel, the skilled trades, the hourly workforce and the union.

Once the committee had reached a consensus on the top 100 candidates, the applicants' names were revealed and then checked against past appraisal ratings. A "competent" rating was a minimum requirement.

(Our pre-screening identified a candidate pool **twice** the number required to fill available openings as Team Coordinators.)

Stage 3: Assessment

Assessment began with one-hour individual interviews by the Kepner-Tregoe organization. This was to determine each candidate's ability to learn and teach rational problem-solving and decision-making techniques.

Assessment continued with a series of individual and team exercises designed to measure each candidate's ability to work in a team environment and to evaluate his or her ability to communicate, orally and in writing, to give and receive feedback, to confront conflict and to plan, organize, delegate and to make balanced choices.

All candidates were observed and evaluated by a team of hourly employees, members of the operating staff and union representatives.

For each skill assessed, a candidate was given a numerical rating. Those who scored the highest overall were selected as Team Coordinators.

These examples demonstrate the use of rational techniques in one aspect—personnel selection—of the planning process. Rationality, however, is only the first criterion that an alternative must meet.

Assuring consistency and integration

At this point we must put the selected alternatives—these options for change—on the firing line. As attractive as they may be on one level, they must still stand up to the test of consistency. Do they work for the **whole** organization? If such and such change is initiated into the system, will it adversely affect this or that group? Will it prove to be a weak link in the transformation chain?

The ''check and balance'' technique proved to be a valuable tool for this sort of assessment. In graphic form it looks like this:

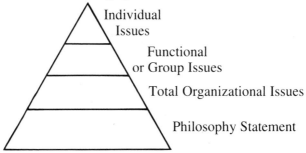

Individual Issues

Functional or Group Issues

Total Organizational Issues

Philosophy Statement

The broad base of the triangle—the philosophy statement—is the foundation of the organization. All changes, all options, and all solutions must be consistent with its principles.

The next layer represents issues that have impact on the total organization. As the triangle draws to its peak, in the third and fourth layers, the focus narrows proportionally, first to the group or to a specific function within the organization, then to issues that affect the individual worker.

The triangle is then separated vertically into the organization's objectives. For the Livonia operation these are, as we have said, product quality, quality of worklife and productivity—the "legs" of our three-legged milking stool—the balanced equation of our ideal organization of the future.

Individual Issues

Functional or Group Issues

Total Organizational Issues

Philosophy Statement

Product   Quality   Productivity
Quality   of
                      Worklife

To pass the test, an alternative for change must meet a double challenge to its consistency—that is, it must work both horizontally and vertically. If it does, it becomes a clear candidate for integration into the transformation process; if the alternative fails at any checkpoint, it must be dropped.

Trust in this approach to developing an overall operating plan grows when those who will be affected by the outcome understand that a given change is a change for the better when it is consistent with an accepted philosophy, when it meets the needs and objectives of the total organization, when it is beneficial to groups and individuals alike, and when, at the same time, it fosters improvement in the organization's stated objectives without doing so at the expense of any of the objectives.

How does this work in a day-to-day issue?

One identifiable issue in the old Livonia operation was a lack of incentive for people to work together. The problem was analyzed using Performance Analysis; the cause turned out to be the absence of any meaningful, positive consequence that would reinforce team effort.

Once understood, the problem became an opportunity for beneficial change. Using Decision Analysis, the Planning Team developed a set of alternative solutions. One alternative was a "team suggestion award" system.

Put to the test of the "check and balance" approach, the proposed system proved inconsistent, and was dropped. While it moved upwards through the triangle with flying colors, it failed at the top: a team suggestion award would effectively foreclose the opportunity for an individual to propose and be rewarded for a personal suggestion.

Furthermore it failed in the test for horizontal consistency and integration. While the award system was consistent with the need to improve product quality and productivity, it worked **against** the interests of quality of worklife: it could be perceived by the individual as both a pressure to participate and as a loss of individual recognition.

The dilemma was solved by implementing a combined system of individual **and** team suggestion awards—a combination that was consistent in all respects—as a functional element of the Business Team approach.

Placed side by side with the many massive issues facing the average organization, one might think the issue we have described as, perhaps, "small potatoes"—something too meager to warrant attention. But the old tale of ". . . For want of a nail, a kingdom was lost . . ." seems especially apt. For the worker on the plant floor, there are no small issues. For those who seek genuine transformation for the better, there are no small issues.

Timing and modification

An unusually successful manager we met some time ago was asked, at the end of a workshop in organizational change, what were the three most important factors for effective reorganization.

"Easy," he said, "Number One **timing**; Number Two **timing**; Number Three **timing**."

When this audience stopped laughing, the impact of the message, of course, remained with us for some time to come.

Our final step in the development of the Livonia plan was to assure ourselves that each alternative for change that had passed the tests for consistency and integration was properly timed for implementation. Some alternatives must, of necessity, be implemented as part of the organization's initial changes. These are the changes that affect basic structure, work-classifications appropriate to the Business Team concept, changes in training and feedback, and systems for selecting personnel who will participate in the new organization.

Other alternatives for change must be implemented **only when the organization is ready to deal with them**. Reorganization abounds in sensitive, even emotional, issues: lines of demarcation in skilled trades . . . issues of mutual trust, such as the elimination of time clocks . . . sophisticated issues based on established performance, such as a gain-sharing program and so on. A well-timed change, prepared through thoughtful planning, will flow into ongoing systems; a poorly timed change will almost surely upset the apple cart of balanced transformation—even, in some instances, to the point of bringing an otherwise finely tuned plan crashing to our feet.

The plan must also provide for appropriate modifications as the new business operation develops. A change implemented at an early stage of transformation may no longer work at a later stage. Perhaps it will need light modification, or wholesale alteration, or even elimination.

We can determine this only through clear communication, measurement and feedback—three elements that must be provided for in the overall operating plan. The total organization must understand what is expected of it, how progress and results are measured and how and why feedback must be an ongoing element of change. Alternatives must be reevaluated, retested using rational processes and resubjected to the demands of consistency and integration. Nothing, in short, can be taken for granted over the long haul of transformation.

Approving the plan

The Planning Team must now present its draft of the overall operating plan to the management and union leadership. It seeks approval of every item, every solution, every alternative.

The task is made easier because a properly designed plan has built-in ingredients to make its contents clear:

. . . a description of initial changes

. . . a time schedule for implementation of alternatives

. . . a description of how the organization will function when all items are implemented

. . . the testing ground of the check-and-balance technique (The technique provides natural break points to obtain appropriate approval with affected groups **during** the plan-making stage.)

. . . support of the analytical and rational processes used in preparing the plan (Out of these can be developed excellent summary reports for review by those interested in the problem-solving information and the objectives and alternatives considered.)

The overall operating plan at Livonia was accepted as proposed by both union and management officials. Because rational process was used in developing the plan, it could be presented in a logical sequence. In presenting the plan, the Livonia Planning Team first identified broad areas in need of change, the specific problems and opportunities within an area of need for change, the causes of problems, the alternatives considered, the objectives to be met and the consistency of solutions included.

Acceptance was also eased because the Planning Team had developed both a means to monitor success of the plan and an implementation timetable that considered the organization's readiness for each alternative. The team also acknowledged that the Livonia overall operating plan, like any plan, may need later modification.

The fact that the plan was overwhelmingly approved was due to all of the factors that led to that decisive moment: the Planning Team members were carefully selected, influential in the group each represented and kept that group informed throughout the planning process . . . thorough analysis preceded planning . . . planning processes were approached rationally . . . and the plan was consistent, integrated and flexible.

REVIEW/GUIDELINES/APPLICATION

TRANSFORMATION: STAGE 10

How An Overall Operating Plan Is Developed

A well-made operating plan is like a good map. It highlights the places to which you are going and tells you how to get there. It outlines alternate routes. It provides options. It gives you a means to measure the distance from here to there. The "map" also has footnotes, explaining why, when and how a change in your trip plans may take place.

A good operating plan also reconciles your company's objectives, making sure that essentials are accounted for and that nothing is overlooked.

A good plan is the result of rational thinking—that is, of thinking that is clear, directed and systematic. A well-trained Planning Team, having already identified areas of needed change, can profitably employ proven rational processes to draw up a plan consistent with the organization's stated philosophy and integrated to benefit all concerned. The Livonia Planning Team used rational techniques learned during its training in problem solving and decision making.

Preparation of a plan is made easier through a three-part process: the development of alternative solutions to stated problems; a testing of these alternatives to evaluate their consistency within the organizational framework; and a determination of how and when a given alternative will be implemented and evaluated for later modification.

Rational processes are used in whatever combination best suits the problem at hand. The Livonia team used Situation Appraisal, Problem Analysis, Decision Analysis and Potential Problem Analysis. Appropriate appraisals and analyses may then be more finely focused to include problems dealing either with human performance or technical/process areas. The purpose of appraisal is to define specific issues at stake; the purpose of analysis is to transform a problem into an opportunity for beneficial change. Then each alternative is evaluated using the check-and-balance technique.

One problem at Livonia—"The Case of the General Foreman" mentioned earlier in this book—combined rational processes with an approach that analyzed the problem and its possible solution in terms of driving forces: a push for implementation versus a restraining force.

The Livonia Planning Team considered the possible alternative of eliminating the level of General Foreman.

This change was in alignment with top management's desire to reduce management layers and with the union's interest in reduced supervision of hourly workers.

Rational process then identified these restraining forces:

. . . Coordination among work teams might be adversely affected.

. . . Work teams would have nowhere to turn for technical assistance in solving problems.

. . . Leaders below the level of General Foreman would have no higher supervision level to which they could advance.

. . . Several well-qualified General Foremen would be excluded from participation in the new organization.

Rational process then identified alternatives that would effectively reduce the restraining forces:

. . . A technical support group was created to help work teams during the more crucial phases of production.

. . . A system of proficiency promotion was developed to advance effective lower-level supervisors in grade, yet allowing them to maintain their same job responsibilities.

. . . Foreman and General Foreman were treated as prime candidates for important supervisory roles in the new organization. No candidate would lose his or her current pay range if selected.

However attractive an alternative solution may be, it must be put to the test of consistency within the context of a **community** of integrated solutions. In short, is that alternative beneficial to the total organization as well as to the group and the individual? Is it consistent with the organization's philosophy? Does it meet the requirements of the company's objectives?

These issues are decided by using checks and balances—graphically represented by this figure:

Individual
Issues
Functional or
Group Issues

Total Organizational Issues

Philosophy Statement

Product   Quality   Productivity
Quality   of
          Worklife

An alternative for change must be consistent **throughout** this context—that is, both horizontally and vertically—if it is to be worthy of implementation.

A selected alternative will work if its implementation is properly timed. A premature change may undermine part or all of the operating plan. Proper timing is equated with that moment when the organization is ready to accept the given change—an issue that is especially important when the change is a sensitive one or one that may trigger emotional responses from the workforce.

A good operating plan also has provisions for possible future modifications of a previously accepted change. Why, when and how a modification should take place is determined by feedback from the persons, systems, or operations affected by that change. If a modification is required, the change must be reevaluated using rational processes and checks and balances for assuring consistency and integration.

The completed plan must finally be presented to the management and union leadership for approval. The more carefully the plan has been assembled, the better is its chances for acceptance. A well made plan will carry clear descriptions of its proposals, an appropriate schedule for their implementation, an assessment of their value to the future organization and sufficient background material to verify their substance and the results of their testing.

The overall operating plan, once approved, is ready for implementation.

Chapter 12

The Operating Plan/Part 1

Supporting the Business Team Approach

Some of us may remember the first appearance of those funny looking, square-bodied, noisy, pioneer automobiles as they chug-chugged along the dusty backroads and cobblestoned streets. "It'll never work!" they said. "Get a horse!" they shouted. "Gol-derned contraption! What'll they think up next?" they exclaimed. (All right, you don't remember, but you have seen movies about them!)

More of us recall those early postage-stamp-sized TV screens, encased in massive pieces of furniture. We had to sit single-file to watch Uncle Milty. "Don't know how they do it," they muttered, "but can't see that there's much future in it."

Even more of us remember John F. Kennedy's mandate to put a man on the moon. "A man on the **moon**?" they whispered in disbelief, "I dunno, maybe they can do it, but we'll never see **that in our** lifetime!"

The growing-up years of many of us were filled with fantastic pipe dreams—those exciting but thoroughly implausible ideas: a rocket ship to explore space . . . a backpacking power unit that could lift a man above the trees . . . Dick Tracy's two-way wrist radio (or was it a miniature TV?) . . . a computer small enough to carry? . . . a calculator the size of a playing card? . . . a camera that actually develops its own pictures, right on the spot? "Why, a running man can't ever break the four-minute mile!" they said.

When a dream becomes a reality, we find ourselves squarely in the middle of movement from "oldthink" to "newthink." We are forced to make a striking shift in our attitudes, beliefs and assumptions. What "will never work" is suddenly working perfectly well in front of our eyes.

A whole mass of our most inbred, stubborn attitudes, beliefs, and assumptions are about people—especially people and their place in organizations:

> "A worker's got to conform! There's no place here for individuality."

> "If a business hierarchy wasn't a good thing, how come the system's been around so long?"

> "Stick to your job. That's what you're here for."

> "Business is business. Nice guys finish last."

> "There's a time for work and a time for play. You're not expected to enjoy yourself from nine to five."

> "Keep your nose clean and you'll get a raise. What more do you want?"

> "Business is civilized warfare. Management's over here . . . the union's over there . . . the consumer's out in left field."

> "Feelings? Intuition? You must be kidding. We trust our data. What more is there?"

Contrasted with those assumptions of the "old" is a whole range of assumptions of the "new:"

> An individual employee knows more about his or her own job than anyone else.

> Most people want to be involved and informed.

> Employees deserve and want a voice in shaping their own destiny.

> A motivated worker is a flexible worker, capable of dealing creatively with a new responsibility.

Worker autonomy, self-actualization and active participation are practical, workable realities.

Expertise in one job does not preclude expertise in another job, however unfamiliar that new role may be at the outset.

Former adversaries can learn to cooperate. Human values transcend winning.

Work can be rewarding in itself, given an ambiance of trust, commitment and mutual support.

A sense of trust, achievement and self-enrichment is a worker's finest reward. Tangible and intangible values can be blended.

Goals and values can be shared. Polarization is a habit that can be broken.

Human resources are our most precious commodity. Their proper development can come only from people working with people, perceiving each other as whole beings.

This is a picture of work on a human scale, of harmonious relationships, of runaway technology bridled to serve the worker—and thus the entire organization—as a tool instead of a tyrant. It is a picture of productive approaches and methods, of balance, compassion and sharing. It is a picture of the spirit underlying an organizational operating plan that embraces the organization as an ensemble, **a true community**, of human beings sharing a common goal.

Rooted in the Livonia statement of operating philosophy are a number of items that were shaped into elements of our operating plan. These are outlined below; their detailed description appears later in this book.

". . . **Together through trust** . . . **and respect** . . ."

- the elimination of distinctions in the work environment between salaried and hourly employees;
- increased responsibility and involvement for all employees;
- increased autonomy for all employees;
- the open sharing of information, including financial data;
- the setting of understandable expectations;

". . . through communication . . ."

- the establishment of team meetings, plant meetings and meetings between those elected to supervise the teams;
- the sharing of key performance indicator reports;
- an accessible, visible management;
- reduced supervision;
- creation of a plant newsletter;
- team structures that foster unimpeded communication;

". . . supportive of employee development . . ."

- the opportunity for all employees to learn all jobs;
- thorough orientation of the workforce;
- the training of all employees in problem solving and decision making;
- the support of skill development through increased responsibilities;
- supportive supervision on all operational levels;

". . . and use of their knowledge and skills . . ."

- workable systems for team and individual suggestions;
- establishment of the concept of "Quality Operator;"
- increased opportunities for responsibility and participation;
- the opportunity to move onward to the role of Assistant Team Coordinator;
- team structure that encourages the use of individual knowledge and skills;

". . . towards the achievement of personal goals . . ."

- a reward system for individual suggestions for improvements;
- the establishment of a system of Pay-for-Knowledge;

- fulfillment of individual needs through increased autonomy;
- the opportunity for transfer among the teams;

". . . production of a high quality product . . ."

- the establishment of statistical process and quality control;
- the integration of production and quality control;
- the training of all employees in quality control;

". . . of a competitive product . . ."

- the upgrading of a product through the Pay-for-Knowledge system and team suggestions for improvement;
- team scrap control;
- team inventory control;
- the preparation of key indicator reports on all cost components;
- the stressing of progress by means of trend reports;

". . . in a clean and safe plant . . ."

- establishment of a housekeeping and safety committee;
- employee involvement in the development and decor of the plant;
- skilled trades employees as team members where appropriate;

". . . our development to be a dynamic process . . ."

- the careful timing of change implementation;
- continued training and development of all employees;
- modifications to be planned by all affected groups;

". . . support from the entire organization . . ."

- the involvement of all groups within the organization—management, union, and workforce—in all stages of the process of transformation;

- integration of support groups.

The organizational changes proposed to and implemented by the Livonia management, union and workforce are illustrations of the scope of the Business Team approach. These are the changes that worked for us. They reflect solutions that were appropriate to our business operations and to the conditions surrounding them. **Their significance lies not in their specifics, which focused on our needs, but on the character and range of solutions that are available to any other organization.**

We have outlined these items (and will explain them in greater detail) as products of a **dynamic** process of transformation. The embracing of such a dynamic process is no more or less than a vehicle for appropriate change. Each organization must design and develop its own approach within that context. An approach must reflect the organization that creates and sustains it: the character of the company, its stage of development, the nature of its human resources and its objectives. Everything else must grow from such seeds.

In developing its own physical environment, its decision-making and problem-solving techniques, its operating systems and procedures, its organizational structure and communication network, each organization will confront the golden opportunity to transform the "old" to the "new" through mutual trust, mutual support, mutual commitment, and the supportive relationships that sustain an unending process, a dynamic process, of improvement.

That this may press us to make a striking shift in our attitudes, beliefs and assumptions about the role of the workforce and the role of the organization should be perceived as an essential first step along the road to significant change for the better. What "will never work" can astonish us all by suddenly working perfectly well.

REVIEW/GUIDELINES/APPLICATION

TRANSFORMATION: STAGE 11

Philosophy . . . Plan . . . Results

The chart on the next page summarizes the items that were developed from the principles of the Livonia statement of philosophy. Since we have already jumped the gun earlier in the book by outlining the positive outcomes of the Business Team approach, their inclusion here, while offering no new information, places the outcomes in the perspective of the actions that caused them. This paints a somewhat more complete picture of the connections between an implemented change and its results.

More important than the specifics, however, is the context in which improvement was generated. What happened at Livonia can happen in any other organization. The ''secret'' of course is not in the details but rather in the dynamic process that served as a fertile soil for the seeds of change. With that in mind, each organization that seeks a more fruitful future can similarly plant the seeds that reflect its own character, resources, needs and objectives.

OPERATING PHILOSOPHY AND SYSTEMS DEVELOPED

TRUST & RESPECT	COMMUNICATION	DEVELOPMENT	KNOWLEDGE AND SKILLS USAGE	PERSONAL GOALS
Elimination of work environment distinctions between salary/hourly.	Team meetings.	Opportunity to learn all jobs.	Team suggestions	Team and individual suggestion awards.
Increased responsibility and involvement.	Plant meetings, Team coordinator (TC) & assistant TC	Orientation	Quality operator concept.	Pay-for-knowledge.
Increased autonomy.	Key performance indicator reports.	Training in problem solving and decision making	Increased responsibility and participation.	Increased autonomy.
Information sharing including financial data.	Accessible and visible management.	Increased responsibilities.	Opportunity to be an assistant team coordinator.	Transfer among teams.
Encourage acceptance of responsibility; set and understand expectations, rather than discipline	Reduced supervision.	Supportive supervision.	Business team structure.	
	Plant newsletter.		Formation of management team.	
	Business team structure.			
	Formation of management team.			

HIGH QUALITY PRODUCT	COMPETITIVE PRODUCT	CLEAN AND SAFE PLANT	DYNAMIC	SUPPORT
Integration of production and quality control.	Pay-for-knowledge.	Housekeeping and safety committee.	Timing of implementation.	Initial involvement of union, management and all affiliated groups.
All employees trained in quality control	Team suggestions.	Involvement in plant development and decor.	Modifications planned by all affected groups.	Continued involvement of all groups.
Statistical process and quality control.	Team scrap control.	Resident skilled trades.	Continuing training and development.	
	Team inventory control.			
	Key indicator report on all cost components.			
	Progress stressed via trend reports.			

RESULTS AFTER TWO YEARS

TRUST & RESPECT	COMMUNICATION	DEVELOPMENT	KNOWLEDGE AND SKILLS USAGE	PERSONAL GOALS
50% reduction in absenteeism	Only one grievance not solved by team or plant.	27% of plant at highest pay rate.	Several hundred percent increase in suggestions and savings.	Several hundred percent increase in suggestion awards.
Grievances in first year equal to what would be expected in one week.	Acceptance of increased responsibility.	Entire plant trained in problem solving and decision making.	97% participation in pay-for-knowledge increases.	27% of the workforce at the highest skill and pay rate.
	Shift in attitudes and perceptions	Continuing training for staff, team coordinators, assistant team coordinators, and quality operators.		

RESULTS AFTER TWO YEARS

HIGH QUALITY PRODUCT	COMPETITIVE PRODUCT	CLEAN AND SAFE PLANT	DYNAMIC	SUPPORT
Significant and consistent improvement in: • Torque control; • Defect reduction; • Process control; • Quality audits; • Customer complaints reduced by 40%; • Warranty reduction each year.	33% increase in machine uptime. 50% reduction controllable cost per engine. 37% reduction in scrap. 100% increase in daily production in first year; 20% in second year. Warranty claims down 56% in first year and 29% in second year. Increased employment over 900.	23% reduction in injuries. 10% improvement in housekeeping index	Additional training scheduled. Further involvement of quality operators planned.	Comments from corporate and union leaders indicate continued and increased support.

Chapter 13

The Operating Plan/Part 2

A New Structure

An organization built around the concept of the small, autonomous, multi-disciplined work group cannot depend on a traditional hierarchical structure. It is inappropriate to the concept. Its flow along functional lines is inconsistent with the concept.

Why is this so? Functional structures at the local plant level are typically divided into production, quality control, material control, personnel, finance and plant engineering. Each of these areas is further divided and subdivided into finer and finer elements. Over time, these smaller divisions habitually generate loyalty to their own objectives, often in opposition to organizational objectives. Small "turfs" are formed; parochialism develops; power struggles are commonplace; added layers of management are instituted to gain a semblance of control.

As a result teamwork erodes, problems become major concerns and areas of responsibility become blurred. More time is spent laying blame than on problem solving. Short-term decisions replace long-range objectives. The system slowly crumbles around the edges.

The concept of the Business Team—with its emphasis on supportive teamwork in an informed environment—has no place in such a structure. Thus the needed change.

As outlined earlier in this book, a structure supportive of the

Business Team concept has several parts: the "building blocks" (the work teams), support systems, a first level of management or supervision, support groups and higher levels of management.

The Business Team

Each small, autonomous work group consists of from eight to fifteen employees set up along product, functional, or geographical lines. The team includes all disciplines that are needed to carry out daily operating responsibilities. The usual distinctions in manufacturing, quality control and material handling are removed by the elimination of job and pay classifications. Each worker in the team is classified as a Quality Operator. Each worker in the team can perform any number of tasks to assure the team's success.

With the elimination of the traditional "this is my job; that's yours" attitude, responsibilities of Quality Operators are widened. A single team is responsible for any number of tasks: meeting production goals, maintaining quality control, posting statistical quality control data, maximizing machine uptime, supervising safety practices, handling material, handling repairs, controlling scrap, supervising preventive maintenance, coordinating the pay-for-knowledge system (more about this later), handling overtime assignments, housekeeping, running the election of Assistant Team Coordinator (explained below), handling daily job placement and rotation, managing feedback, counseling other team members, training new team members and interfacing with other teams.

It is this assimilation of all functions into the Business Team that effectively does away with "turf" protection, parochialism, power struggles, a loss of objectives, boredom and the deadly feeling of being an inert cog in a vast, impersonalized wheel.

The shift from single-task orientation to multi-function responsibility is not easy for the traditionally trained workforce. Initial concern, anxiety, even fear, however, are replaced in time by a sense of self-fulfillment, achievement, advancement and—that rarest of plant visitors—pleasure in one's craft.

The Assistant Team Coordinator

This position is created to assist the team in accepting the responsibility for day-to-day, work-related tasks. He or she is an hourly employee elected by the peer group to supervise daily job assignments, facilitate problem-solving meetings, and administer support systems that help the team accomplish its missions. He or she also assumes many of the more routine daily functions previously performed by a foreman.

Support Systems

The purpose of a support system is to help the Business Team achieve its objectives of meeting production goals, maintaining quality control, increasing machine uptime and handling daily job replacement and rotation.

In this sense the Assistant Team Coordinator, through working shoulder to shoulder with the team members, is an important element of their support systems.

Other elements of the support systems are a uniform job classification, the pay-for-knowledge system, training programs, team meetings and an award system for employee suggestions.

(a) **The uniform job classification**, as we have already mentioned, substitutes a single classification—the Quality Operator—for traditional job labels describing functions, experience or specific skills.

(b) **The pay-for-knowledge system** is implemented to encourage and reward employees for learning new skills that enable them to participate effectively in the Business Team. Under this system an individual earns pay increases by learning all the job functions on his or her team and, later, by transferring to another team and learning all of **those** jobs. In this way the individual as well as the team is rewarded by capitalizing on the strong motivation that drives the individualism of the American worker.

(c) Every employee is given extensive **training in problem solving and decision making**. This training significantly eases the tasks confronting the team. Training also includes team building exercises to promote group cooperation. The trainers are drawn from the ranks of the first-level supervisors.

(d) **Team meetings** are held once each week, for one hour, on company time. This environment is conducive to problem solving and decision making; the meetings also provide a vehicle for open communication between the teams and the rest of the organization.

(e) **Suggestion awards** are shared among all members of a team, including the team supervisor (see below), thereby encouraging mutually supportive work processes. Awards are generally given for suggestions on ways to improve product quality, increase productivity and implement more effective safety measures.

The First Level of Management

Because of the increased responsibility passed on to the Business Team and the Assistant Team Coordinator, there is no longer a need for a foreman or general foreman. This does not, however, preclude the need for someone to assist the team in its development, to serve as a liaison between the team and the top management group and to assure the accomplishment of team goals—at least until the team is ready to act on its own.

This role falls to the **Team Coordinator**—a salaried employee selected specifically for his or her technical competence and leadership skills.

In addition to providing the team the autonomy to mature without undue interference, the Team Coordinator may also be responsible for the growth of other Business Teams, depending on the rate of growth of the first team and the complexity of its responsibilities. To prepare for these important functions, the Team Coordinator is given additional training in communication skills, small-group facilitation and advanced training in problem solving and decision making.

Support Groups

A support group is a team of specialists whose job is to assist Business Teams as the need arises. Although one member of a given Business Team may be a skilled electrician, for example, a group of electronics specialists may be called upon to solve a particularly troublesome problem that is beyond that person's skills. This system of mutual support maintains Business Team autonomy while providing a reliable and available source of help.

Higher Levels of Management

The higher level of management is the **Top Management Group**, organized to form its own Business Team. Although the team includes specialists in manufacturing, quality control, personnel, finance, material management and process engineering, each member is encouraged to become familiar with **all** of the responsibilities of the group.

The top management team reports to the **Plant Manager**, who functions as its Team Coordinator to assist the team in its growth and development.

This uniformity of structure throughout the organization extends as well to the team's training, which is identical to that of all other Business Teams in terms of problem solving and decision making, using the same rational processes.

Like other teams the Top Management Group has several support systems to encourage its development. One, for example, is a team appraisal system that evaluates individuals on their cooperative approach to team issues and on their progress in expanding their knowledge beyond a given specialized area. (The process for selecting its members appears later in this book.)

The Total Structure

These descriptions of the total organization illustrate a degree of consistency and solidity, from the plant floor to the manager's office, that in all aspects reflects the spirit of the organization's statement of philosophy. The uniformity of structure, built cohesively around the concept of the autonomous Business Team, is self-evident.

Equally evident is the vast difference between this structure and that of the traditional hierarchical organization. The way workers are organized has become a critical function of the success or failure of American industry. At this point in our industrial evolution—when traditional means no longer work to maintain the spiritual and economic health of the average American company—the existence of a workable alternative is cause for a degree of hope for survival, so sadly lacking for so long.

REVIEW/GUIDELINES/APPLICATION

TRANSFORMATION: STAGE 12

Blocks, Support, and Supervision (Structuring the New Organization)

The traditional organizational structure is inappropriate for and unsupportive of the Business Team concept.

This is due to the traditional segmenting of the organization into functional lines (production, quality control, and so on) that, in turn, break down into smaller, self-protective "turfs." As a result of these separated allegiances and the unproductive power struggles linked to them, teamwork erodes, problems mount and responsibilities become blurred. In the process the organization's prime objectives give way to short-term decisions and stop-gap problem solving.

Because the Business Team concept can flourish only in an arena of supportive teamwork, in an informed environment, the traditional organizational structure must be replaced by a workable substitute. This new structure consists of five levels: the Business Teams (the "building blocks"), support systems, a first level of management, support groups and higher levels of management.

The Business Team is a small, autonomous group whose members are trained to perform a wide variety of tasks, all aimed at completing a specific organizational goal. This broad spreading out of responsibility is in sharp contrast to the traditional single-task orientation found in American industry. With the elimination of job and pay classifications, each member becomes a Quality Operator, working in a mutually supportive group to achieve a common goal.

The Business Teams are helped by **support systems**, created to assist each team in reaching its objectives. The first element of these support systems is a person, the **Assistant Team Coordinator**, who acts as a general supervisor to facilitate the team's work, processes and goals. The other supportive elements are systems:

(a) **The uniform job classification**, with its opportunity to learn and carry out a number of interrelated jobs, helps eliminate traditional parochialism and artificial barriers among workers. At the same time it offers the worker a means toward a higher degree of self-fulfillment and self-actualization that was not before possible.

(b) **The pay-for-knowledge system** is a direct reflection of the multi-faceted team itself, encouraging diversity and the acquisition of new skills as ends in themselves yet clearly tied to responsive pay increases as the individual grows.

(c) Tasks and team missions are greatly facilitated by **training in problem solving and decision making**, using the same rational processes that inform organizational transformation at every stage of change.

(d) **Team meetings** create a welcome arena for additional teamwork, yet place the group in closer contact with the rest of the organization.

(e) Mutual support within the Business Team is tied to and reflected by the fair sharing of **suggestion awards**—a material, public acknowledgement of individual and team concerns for product quality, productivity, and safety.

The creation of the positions of Assistant Team Coordinator and **Team Coordinator**—the latter considered as the first level of management or supervision—effectively does away with tasks formerly assigned to a foreman and general foreman, thus eliminating these positions within the new structure. The Team Coordinator assists team development, works with the team toward accomplishment of its goals and serves as a communication link between the team and top management.

Support Groups are teams of specialists. As the need arises they may be called upon to assist a Business Team whose own expertise may still be insufficient to solve a particularly difficult problem.

The Top Management Group occupies the higher levels of management within the new organizational structure. Like all groups at other levels of the company, it too is formed as a Business Team with a Team Coordinator. In this case, however, the group members are management specialists (in manufacturing, quality control, and so on), and the Coordinator is the **Plant Manager**. Also like all other Business Teams, members of the Top Management Group are encouraged to familiarize themselves with all responsibilities represented within the group.

The significant difference between this new organizational structure and the typical traditional American industrial structure lies in two areas: in its refusal to accept past organizational practices an an unquestioned ''given'' and in its willingness to accept and develop an alternative founded in the previously unmined riches of the organization's own human resources—its most precious, yet unrealized, commodity.

Chapter 14

From Operating Plan To Implementation: New Systems in a New Environment

The dynamic process of organizational transformation hardly lends itself to a neat chronological order of events! Conditions change constantly; the process responds to conditions; valuable suggestions and suggested modifications flow in and out of the process like fish in a stream; growth and development come in all shapes and sizes, appearing when they will. Planning and implementation, strategy and tactics overlap one another, perfectly resistant to neatness.

Some aspects of the process still preserve some sort of linearity. This is especially so of the simultaneous implementation of necessary first steps (major structural elements, for example) put into place in one broad move, while supporting organizational changes are implemented as the company is ready to accept them.

Support elements that must be in place at the start of implementation are mainly related to systems that encourage communication, provide for participation, demonstrate management's commitment to change, and foster growth and the visible progress of the Business Teams.

While we must now wade lightly in the waters of "implementation" (a subject that deserves, and gets, its own section of the book) what follows should be understood as the form ("final" at the mo-

129

ment of implementation) of support systems shaped during the making and approval of the overall operating plan.

The Physical Environment

The physical environment at Livonia was changed to eliminate separate parking lots and dining facilities for the supervisory staff and the hourly workforce. We also eliminated other symbols or "badges" that denote some sort of distinction in rank or hierarchy, particularly the wearing of white shirts and ties by management personnel. This was a visible sign that management's agreement to a broad-based **team** concept, including the environment and the dress "code," was a direction backed by action.

Further physical changes included a plant library, team meeting rooms on the plant floor, and offices for union representatives. Plant decor was planned with an eye toward more pleasant surroundings and a neat, business-like ambiance.

A Visible, Approachable Management

Systems to encourage management visibility, approachability and credibility are absolutely necessary at the onset of organizational change. This encourages open, honest communication up, down and sideways within the organization. Individuals and groups must feel comfortable discussing any concern with any member of the organization at any time.

Although the development of mutual comfort and familiarity is to a great extent dependent on personal empathy and communication skills, certain steps can be taken to encourage its growth:

> . . . The Plant Manager and the Top Management Group must make conscious efforts to spend considerable time on the plant floor, getting to know individuals and their concerns in their work environment.

> . . . The Plant Manager, along with responsible staff members, Team Coordinators, Assistant Team Coordinators, union representatives, and Quality Operators should make daily safety and housekeeping tours of the plant.

> (At Livonia more than a few workers were flabbergasted to see the Plant Manager picking up newspapers, beverage cans, and discarded lunch bags in the parking

lot. They dubbed him "the most highly paid janitor in America," but the point was clearly made by his housekeeping concerns for **his** workplace.)

. . . Special task forces should be set up to address specific environmental concerns as they come up: the criteria and equality of advancement, provisions for the suggestion program, services to the employees (parking, cafeteria, rest rooms) and so on.

These committees comprise staff, union representatives, Team and Assistant Team Coordinators, and Quality Operators.

. . . The plant staff should participate actively in all team meetings.

Basic Communication

Systems must be established at the outset of plant operations for broad-based communication and performance feedback. These serve as a means by which the entire workforce is informed of its progress, a vehicle for two-way dialogue, and a method for identifying and responding to early concerns of the Business Teams. Practical and reliable systems include the following:

. . . weekly team meetings, for one hour, on company time;

. . . daily meetings of the supervisory staff, with participation by the union and Quality Operators, to discuss overall operations;

. . . weekly staff meetings to discuss progress and to coordinate activities;

. . . monthly coordination meetings between the staff and the Team and Assistant Team Coordinators to demonstrate mutual concern with and resolution of problems;

. . . a system of performance progress reports to reinforce expectations, handle feedback, and provide recognition of Business Team progress;

. . . a weekly plant newsletter, including published acknowledgement of progress, accepted suggestions, and awards;

. . . and, finally, a regular schedule of quarterly plant meetings, focusing, as do other regular meetings, on the organization's progress toward long-term goals.

Basic Training

Throughout Livonia's process of transformation from the "old" to the "new," participants in the actualization of change depended heavily on proven, rational techniques designed to facilitate problem solving and decision making. Their training eased the tasks they faced at every stage of organizational development.

In the tightly interlocked structure that supports the Business Team concept, this uniform training program must extend to the workforce as well. Consequently, the onset of plant operations occurs simultaneously with this training, adapted to group participation, to facilitate team building and the development of each work group. This uniformity of approach, from the plant floor to management's offices, guarantees a mutually shared attitude toward problems and decisions, and a shared language in the search for their resolution.

To supplement this basic training, each Business Team member in our plant took part in a team-building training session and was given the opportunity to tear down and rebuild a complete engine. Team Coordinators received supplemental training in facilitating group problem-solving and decision-making meetings.

Employee Participation

Changes in participative decision making center around the involvement of appropriate parties in appropriate decisions—for instance, the inclusion of union and hourly employees on assessment teams that select salaried Team Coordinators—a prime example of fair participation, shared concerns and widened responsibilities.

Hourly, union and management employees at Livonia worked together in small groups during all phases of implementation. In selecting Team Coordinators they reviewed application forms to narrow the candidate pool. Once the candidate pool was narrowed, union, management, and hourly employees were trained as assessment teams and observed Team Coordinator candidates write reports, make presentations, work in a team environment and handle a discipline situation. Candidates were selected based on a consensus of numerical scores developed by the assessment teams.

Candidate selection was only one area of many that included hourly employees and union officials in the decision-making process. Wherever possible appropriate people were involved in a process that would affect their work lives, thus giving them a controlling voice for the first time. During implementation, hourly and union employees presented the orientation programs and trained employees, including supervisors, in problem solving and decision making. As members of Business Teams, hourly employees decided how the job would be covered on a daily basis, how employees would rotate among the jobs and how overtime would be coordinated.

A number of additional support systems are implemented at the outset of operations and then modified over time. These are designed to develop fully as the business teams mature and as input is received from the teams and management.

Pay-for-Knowledge

A pay-for-knowledge compensation system was established for hourly employees at the Livonia plant, giving them pay increases depending on the number of jobs they learned on their Business Team. Advancement to the top rate of pay was achieved when an hourly employee learned all the jobs on two Business Teams. Pay-for-knowledge rewarded employee development and flexibility within the business team and replaced the traditional pay classification system wherein rewards are tied primarily to seniority.

With the pay-for-knowledge concept adopted for a one-year trial period, employees overwhelmingly approved the system after this time, as they found that it was fairly administered and did in fact reward appropriate behavior.

Several adjustments were made to the system during the course of the first year—for example in the criteria for advancement in assembly and machining business teams. The key indicator of percentage of employees at each pay level showed that assembly employees could progress through the pay levels much more easily than machining employees. Analysis indicated the true cause of this situation: machining jobs within a team were not as closely related and required greater training time. To assure fairness in the pay-for-knowledge system, a joint union-management-hourly employee committee redesigned the criteria to provide equal opportunity to **all** Livonia employees.

Measurement and Appraisal Systems

To evaluate team operations we developed key performance indicators, charted both on a trend basis and in table form. This information was passed on to all employees each day and summarized at the end of each week. We also established team appraisals, replacing the traditional boss-subordinate appraisal process commonly found in plant operations.

Reward Systems

As our process evolved, changes in reward systems included implementation of team suggestion awards with provisions to include the Team Coordinator. Pay-for-knowledge, key indicators, and team suggestions were viewed as necessary steps to an eventual system of gain-sharing. The overall objective throughout was to provide each team with the means to influence pay based on performance in key measurable areas.

Policy Interpretation and Application

This area was handled by a plant committee consisting of union, workforce and management representatives, replacing the traditional unilateral control by management alone.

The Union Contract

Over time the discipline and grievance emphasis was changed to stress prevention of unacceptable behavior through a clear understanding of mutually shared expectations. Prior to any formal action both the team and the union had the opportunity to involve themselves in the procedure. In addition the wage agreement was amended to allow for a pay-for-knowledge system, replacing the traditional wage and classification structure.

Quality Control

To maximize the prevention of product defects we replaced traditional checking systems with a sophisticated system of statistical quality control. This was initially implemented by that section of the Quality Control Staff we called the Floor Inspection Team, made up of Quality Operators. This responsibility was gradually shifted to production Business Teams as they matured enough to undertake training in statistical quality control.

Promotion Systems

The general foreman level was eliminated and there were thirty-seven percent fewer team coordinators than there would have been foremen. Selection to the position of Team Coordinator was made from the sixth and seventh levels (formerly foreman and general foreman) in the organization. This allowed qualified individuals from both groups to apply for this new position and, when selected, to maintain their former pay range and scale. This system not only facilitated acceptance of the Team Coordinator position by former general foremen but also created a much needed proficiency promotion system.

Formerly, supervisors doing an excellent job had to be promoted from the job of supervising hourly employees in order to be rewarded. Under the new system Team Coordinators at the sixth level who performed effectively for two or more years with two or more Business Teams received a proficiency promotion to seventh-level Team Coordinator. Thus the organization rewarded competent Team Coordinators without changing their job responsibilities.

Communication and Feedback

The communication and feedback network, implemented from the start of operations, should be modified as the need for change arises. At Livonia, for example, a portion of the performance feedback system developed into a weekly ten-page key indicator report measuring twenty-eight major indicators related to cost, schedule and environment.

The initial report was developed and prepared by salaried employees. As of this writing, the key indicator report has grown to measure forty indicators and is currently developed, formatted and processed by hourly employees using personal computers. The key indicators currently measured at Livonia include:

A. **Productivity**

- Schedule Attainment (Average Pieces Per Day)
- Units Shipped Per Day
- Inventory (Finished)
- Repair Inventory
- Total Inventory Cost
- Engines Produced Per Employee
- Direct Hours Per Engine Produced
- Indirect Hours Per Engine Produced

- Daily Scrap
- Scrap Per Engine
- Machine Reliability
- Machine Use
- Composite Use Efficiency
- Maintenance Labor Per Engine
- Maintenance Supplies Per Engine
- Washer Concentrate Usage
- Hydraulic Oil Usage
- Electricity (Kilowatts Per Engine)
- Coolant Usage Per Engine
- Overtime As A Percentage Of Regular Hours
- Premium Shipments

B. **Quality**

- Quality Index (Specification)
- Quality Index (Functional)
- Quality Index Composite
- Defects Per Engine Produced
- Defects Per Engine Dynamometer
- Percentage Of Engines O.K. Through Hot Test
- Engine Pulls
- Warranty Costs

C. **Industrial relations**

- Absenteeism, Daily, Controllable
- Absenteeism, Total
- Grievances
- Housekeeping Index
- Total Injuries
- Number Of Actual Reportable Injuries Per 200,000 Hours
- Suggestion Frequency (Team)
- Suggestion Frequency (Individual)
- Percent Of Pay-For-Knowledge Levels Attained
- Quality Of Worklife Survey Results

Meetings

As our workplace transformation evolved, the Business Teams at Livonia expressed a need to be informed about progress of the plant as a whole and about future plans of the organization. This led to the scheduling of a plant business meeting every three or four months, replacing the team meeting that would normally have occurred that week. Information at the plant business meeting was presented by various members of the plant staff.

Summary: Timing and Precautions

Industrial change encompasses a range of implementations—some immediate, others added as the organization is ready for them, still others set in place but modified with experience. Because implementation of change is a complex web of actions taken, certain precautions are in order and specific moves must be pre-planned with exceptional care.

REVIEW/GUIDELINES/APPLICATION

TRANSFORMATION: STAGE 13

Working With New Concepts In A New Workplace

An organization that has accepted the challenge of total transformation for the better is faced with a broad range of changes in structure, in its work environment and in its systems and operations. Some of these changes must be implemented at the start of operations in order to encourage communication, provide for true participation among its personnel, show that top leadership can back up its words with action and create a fertile soil in which the Business Teams can mature.

Other changes can be introduced only when the evolving organization is ready to accept them. Still others may be implemented at an early stage but subjected to modification after they have been carefully monitored.

At all times, and in all instances, the leadership must remain aware of how timing—of initial implementation and of later modifications—can either support or undermine the growth of the new organization. Every aspect of systems and operations, in every area, and involving all personnel, must be evaluated continuously.

This crucial task is facilitated and made entirely practical by continual feedback from and open, two-way communication with all employees. What is rare, if not nonexistent in the traditional hierarchical organization, becomes commonplace among people working together as autonomous, responsible teams in a supportive environment, interfacing with systems designed to reflect that support.

From the outset of Livonia operations, the Business Team concept was supported by significant changes in the physical environment, the visibility of management, basic communication and basic training for the entire workforce.

Artificial, yet traditional, barriers between the workforce and the supervisory staff were removed. We dressed alike, parked our cars in the same lot, ate together and met face-to-face on the plant floor and in regularly scheduled meetings. We became a community of people, pulling together toward a common goal: the survival of the organization and the psychological and economic well-being of everyone in it. We were joining in an effort to put behind us, once and for all, the adversarial days of "us versus them" and of the "I win, you lose" mentality.

We believed in and implemented communication systems involving every employee in the plant. We spoke openly of our plans, concerns, problems, successes and progress. We settled issues together, drawing on our organizational training in rational approaches to problem solving and decision making.

We believed in and implemented appropriate participation in these settlements, making sure that those affected by a change, modification or decision took part in that process or, at the very least, were fully informed at every stage. In this way we dealt with our pay-for-knowledge system, our measurement and appraisal systems, reward systems, training, policy interpretation and application, the union contract, quality control, selection decisions and our communication and feedback network.

Chapter 15

The Process Of Implementation

Just as a rational process for planning is more important than the details of a specific plan, the process of implementation is more important than the specific changes implemented. This reality having been driven home by first-hand observation of the problems met in other plants—all due to error of implementation—the Livonia Planning Team devoted special attention to this stage of transformation. To meet the cautious standards established by the team, implementation at Livonia was separated into the six basic steps of orientation, training, systems change, timing, measurement and modification. As training and systems change are covered separately, this chapter will highlight orientation, timing, measurement and modification.

Following plan approval by the union and management, the leadership initiated a two-stage orientation program. This was designed to allow potential Livonia employees the opportunity to understand the new operating environment and to make a knowledgeable choice concerning their decision to participate in the new workplace. (This workforce with an average seniority of approximately twenty years consisted of employees from both the Livonia Engine Plant and the Downtown Engine Facilities.)

The first stage of orientation—a three-hour presentation by the Planning Team, union leaders and management leaders—consisted of an overview of the major changes that would occur at Livonia. As a

140

result of this information, employees either expressed an interest in learning more about the Livonia Plant or indicated that they did not wish to be a part of the new venture. At this point over 98% of the employees elected to continue orientation.

The second stage of orientation began with a visit to the Livonia Engine Plant for a first-hand view of the new technology in operation and continued when all employees were given an opportunity to work in small groups to solve a problem and make a decision. This was followed by a complete and detailed eight-hour explanation of the Business Team Approach, presented to a somewhat skeptical workforce by a united front of management and the union. At this stage employees were invited to ask specific questions concerning pay rate, team makeup, initial job assignments and so on.

As discussed earlier in this book, the gist of the discussion was open communication, freely accepting the skepticism of some and eschewing the idea that all the answers were known. In fact, we said we did not even know all the questions.

Following an intense question-and answer session, more than 82% of the remaining workforce chose to become a part of the Livonia process. From this candidate pool, employees were selected on a seniority basis. Although this high acceptance rate was due in large part to the quality of the message to the workforce—that is, as an expression voiced by a unified, representative planning group—other elements were also responsible for this strong beginning. Chief among these was a situation that clearly promoted voluntary action by the worker.

The opportunity to volunteer at Livonia was of course facilitated by the shut-down, renovation and restart of our plant. Had this not been the case, more creativity would have been needed to retain the voluntary nature of our improvement program.

As forecasted in the introduction at the orientation session, due to cost reduction and quality improvements the demand for an engine, never before successfully produced, increased dramatically. Employment at the Livonia Plant rose from 440 to 800 to 1200 to 1400 and continues to grow.

Timing

Following orientation and training, system changes are made. These changes must be timed to protect the organization from being overwhelmed.

An example of timing comes from the implementation of the systems change to a pay-for-knowledge compensation scheme. The employees were aware that pay-for-knowledge would be in effect when they came to the Livonia plant on the first day of work. When they reported to the Livonia Plant they all had one job classification, "quality operator." When they reported to the Livonia plant all employees were paid the same rate of pay and understood that that rate of pay would change pursuant to learning more jobs in the plant. Employees were placed on business teams in jobs consistent with their previous job classification. For example, a job setter under the old job classification system was assigned to a business team and his first job assignment was that of a job setter. Job rotation was programmed to begin only after an individual business team was producing an acceptable number of engines at an acceptable quality and cost level. This protected the plant from mass-confusion should job rotation begin prematurely in business teams.

Measurement

Once changes are made a system of measurement must be in place to assure that the changes are working properly. As previously discussed, key indicators were used by the business teams and by the overall organization to monitor the change process. The inequities in the pay-for-knowledge level attainment between assembly and machining would never have come to light and been corrected, if percent attainment had not been a key indicator monitored by the Livonia plant.

In addition to providing measurement, the key indicators were essential in structuring meaningful team meetings. The key indicator reports are reviewed at the beginning of every team meeting so the team concentrates on problems in order of priority. Key indicators are fed back to the business teams in a fashion to facilitate problem solving and decision making. For example, the information displayed below is the detail which would accompany a trend chart in the weekly scrap key indicator report.

From the detailed information the team could ascertain that its performance has improved from year to date figures and is far exceeding budget and last year's experience. However, if you are a member of a block team, you would know that your department is still generating $2.68 worth of scrap per engine. Assuming that this is the highest priority performance problem in the 40 key indicator areas, the team would start its problem-solving activity knowing the part number that generated the scrap, the operation where the scrap was observed, the quantity of material scrap and the defect for which the material was rejected. With this information the team has the basic

LIVONIA ENGINE PLANT
"WEEKLY SCRAP REPORT"

DEPARTMENT	BUSINESS TEAM	SCRAP PER ENGINE WEEK	SCRAP PER ENGINE Y T D	SCRAP PER ENGINE BUDGET	SCRAP PER ENGINE LAST YEAR
1712	BLOCK	2.68	2.87	4.00	4.71

HIGH DOLLAR SCRAP CHARGES

DESCRIPTION	PART	DEFECTIVE OPERATION	QUALITY DEFECT	COST	DEFECT DESCRIBED
BLOCK	0161869	050/050	72	5231.66	OVERSIZE BEARING

information to accurately describe the problem and to use the rational problem-solving methodology to eliminate the scrap problem.

In addition to monitoring the performance of the improvement plan and providing data for problem solving and decision making, measurement also provides constant reinforcement and recognition of improved performance. This allows teams to see, understand and intrinsically appreciate their improved performance.

Milestones—those small successes met along the way—must be recognized, acknowledged and communicated to the entire organization. This is necessary food while intrinsic satisfaction evolves. This "food" need not be rich fare; the simplest form of acknowledgement is enough if it is timely and offered genuinely.

At Livonia, milestones related to sustained, superior team performance and to valuable individual suggestions for improvement. Those acknowledged received a free breakfast, donuts and coffee, small momentos imprinted with the plant logo, an article about them in the plant newsletter, or some similar form of recognition. Though not "big" in size or material value, such forms of acknowledgement are indeed big as a communicative gesture, as a mark of consistent awareness of a job well done, as a visible action taken within a context of mutual support.

Modification

At Livonia, measurements confirmed that improvements were achieved and triggered the next phase of advancement. An organization will generally progress and develop until it reaches a plateau. This point, or just before, is the moment to implement the next major step of change or to modify the plan for change.

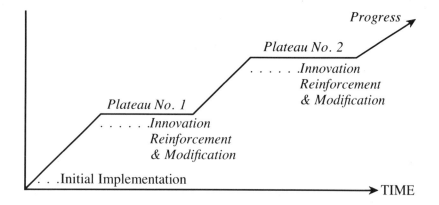

If the leadership is truly in touch with the organization and measurements are well designed, long (static) plateaus can be replaced by a steady continuum of change:

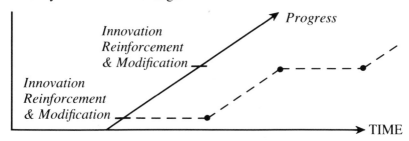

Like the proper timing of change implementation, modifications of in-place systems must be consistent within the context of the total organization and, moreover, must be designed by those affected.

In summary, the purpose of the implementation process is to institutionalize the change process that occurred first with the Planning Team. Following that, individual business teams and support teams, relying on team work, employee development, rational analysis and common purpose begin a comprehensive improvement of quality, productivity and quality of worklife. To support this, the Planning Team had created an organization and environment free from as many obstacles as possible.

The orientation and training for employees at Livonia paralleled the enlightenment and training phase of the Planning Team. Although all plant employees did not have the opportunity to tour other facilities, the Planning Team shared experiences, lessons learned and reasons behind inclusion of various alternatives into the overall operating plan.

As a business or support team became a team in reality, the group developed its own mission supporting the overall operating philosophy. Their mission became a rallying cry and a direct contributor to the entire change process.

The supporting mission can only be developed when a team is ready. Once written and understood, alignment of all individuals on a team toward the accomplishment of a common purpose consistent with the overall operating philosophy is possible. Once a business team or support team adopted its own supportive mission, objectives developed by the team based on key performance indicators naturally followed. Once objectives have been accomplished, they are reestablished and the on-going improvement process becomes a way of doing business.

REVIEW/GUIDELINES/APPLICATION

TRANSFORMATION: STAGE 14

Assuring Successful Implementation

The new implementation process, like the planning process that preceded it must be handled with extreme care. New structures and new systems however are of course meaningless as disembodied **things**. They require a committed human force to move them from abstraction to reality. This means that business teams and support teams must experience the same processes as does the Planning Team: the step-by-step assimilation of orientation, training, team building, enlightenment, philosophy, objectives, alignment, implementation and modification. In this perspective the Planning Team will then have served as a microcosm—literally, a "world" in miniature—for the entire organization.

In Chapter 3 we jumped ahead in our narrative to preview the sense of disorientation that we anticipated in a skeptical workforce confronted with a radical shift from the "old" to the "new:"

> They were worried about pay, seniority, and transfer rights. They were fearful about the implications of fewer available jobs at Livonia. Coming from a traditionally adversarial environment, both salaried and hourly employees suspected management or the union of selling out. With their history of neglect, the workers were suspicious of an innovative social program, anxious about a changed hierarchy within the plant, and wary of misplacing their trust. 'Why should I believe you?' and 'We've heard all this before' were persistent—and understandable—responses at the orientation sessions.

An organization's leadership, committed to transformation for the better, can do no less than to confront these real concerns in a full group session. Given the history of American industry's adversarial relationships, the workers' perceptions of "how things really are" are scathingly accurate.

This is a situation that a united management-labor leadership must turn around. It must treat worker alienation as real. It must treat dissatisfaction on the plant floor as real. It must acknowledge these realities openly and honestly if there is to be a start to genuine two-way communication between leadership and workforce. It must do away with its own lack of credibility by becoming credible.

Transformation is a concept that is likely to be far better received than other attempts to improve an organization, mainly due to the early involvement of the union and hourly workforce as members of the Planning Team. This commitment on the part of the leadership to a democratic voice and to participative planning will not dissolve skepticism in one single act, but it will go far in establishing mutual trust and compassionate communication. The content of the leadership's message and the sincerity with which it is delivered to the workforce will determine the rate of progress of the evolving organization.

Consequently the objectives of an orientation program are fourfold:

- to discuss past errors in the context of future hopes

- to provide a basic understanding of the overall plan for transformation

- to develop trust and credibility

- to give the entire workforce the means and opportunity to make an informed decision about its involvement in the new organization

    At Livonia our orientation was done in two stages: the first, a general overview for the entire workforce; the second, a detailed review of our plan for those who wished to hear more of what we had in mind. Attendance at both meetings was voluntary, a point in harmony with our business philosophy of democratic participation.

Stage 1: A Brief Overview Meeting for the Entire Workforce

Purpose: to expose all prospective employees to our general approach to the new organization; and to begin to develop an environment of trust and credibility.

Strategy: By involving the union, management and Planning Team, we demonstrated the cooperative nature of our approach. This helped to dispel the initial distrust of the concept as simply another management ploy to increase productivity at the workers' expense.

Content: This overview was presented in a two-hour meeting conducted by the Planning Team with assistance from union and management leaders. It explained the key changes in the overall operating plan, contrasting them with parallel elements in the existing organization.

The first Livonia orientation was given to over 2,000 employees in groups of 100 to 150. Following a question-and-answer period, each employee was given a copy of our statement of overall operating philosophy. Those who were interested in more detail signed up for the in-depth Stage 2 orientation session.

Result: At the end of Stage 1 orientation the workforce appeared to be cautiously optimistic. Over 98% of the 2,000 workers signed up to attend the detailed orientation session. Their questions, however, indicated a substantial residue of skepticism.

Stage 2: A Detailed Review of the Transformation Plan

Purpose: to explain the mechanics of our approach, to continue the development of credibility and to provide a team experience for all participants.

Strategy: A continued presentation of the new concept by a united management-labor group helps to solidify an environment of mutual trust in which goals are shared equally in a cooperative effort.

The team building exercise is a sample of what is possible when workers participate in small-group tasks and of the value of group decision making in terms of improved choices and commitment.

The overview of the training process helps to

dispel self-doubts about one's capacity to function and participate as a valuable member of a business team.

Content: The union representative, the Planning Team and the team facilitator presented an eight-hour review. The meeting was conducted outside the work environment in an informal classroom setting for groups of 30 to 40 employees.

The Planning Team spoke of its tours to other plants, what it had observed there, the lessons it had learned as a result of these visits and how these insights were incorporated into the plan. The Team then outlined its training and the evolution of the organization's statement of philosophy. This was followed by a repetition of the key changes in the operating plan and their contrast with elements of the existing organization.

During the question-and-answer period the team answered **all** questions concerning the plan.

At the end of the review participating employees were split into teams of five or six people and took part in an organization-development team exercise. This taste of small-group functioning was followed by a preview of planned training in problem solving and decision making as an aid in promoting work as a team.

The orientation concluded with a review, by the plant manager, of the economic necessity for comprehensive and integrated change. The review described market trends, productivity trends, barriers to free trade and the need for an approach to meet these challenges. The presentation linked quality, productivity and the current threat to industrial survival to an approach that stresses teamwork, employee development and democratic participation to complement capital investment.

The session ended with an extensive question-and-answer period.

Employees were then given an opportunity to sign up for one week of training in problem solving and decision making if they decided to work in the new organization. Those who chose not to participate were placed elsewhere in the Cadillac organization.

Since the company's training investment is substantial and the commitment to participate therefore binding, it is essential that each prospective employee be **fully** informed, and that all his or her questions be answered completely. The presenters must thus be thoroughly versed in how the new approach affects the individual worker in every respect: salary, job classifications, seniority, performance expectations and so on. There is no other route to an **informed** choice.

Result: This detailed orientation clearly illustrated how each employee would be affected through involvement in the new organization. As a result, 82% of the nineteen hundred workers attending the second orientation session chose to accept "the Livonia opportunity."

The plant was staffed with those who volunteered, by seniority within traditional pay classifications. This selection method assured the presence of needed skills while acknowledging length of service to the organization.

We cannot overstress the importance of a thorough and sincere orientation process as the first step of implementation. At each step of the way what occurs must be fully consistent with a philosophy of direct and open communication; of a visible, accessible and committed leadership; of democratic participation; of free choice; and of the willingness to listen completely, respond honestly and share equally.

After planned changes are communicated, they must be implemented in an appropriate time sequence. Enough change must be made initially to overcome resistance to change, but too much change at one time can overcome the organization's capacity to absorb the change and maintain performance.

Measurement assured appropriate and timely implementation, as well as modification of the overall improvement plan. It is the leadership's responsibility to help the total organization reach its full potential through sensitive planning and careful timing of change implementation. One aspect of the plant's forward movement was reflected in management's handling of plateaus—those stages of development during which a contained set of changes "settle in," having been tried, reinforced and modified.

Shortly after Livonia's first year of operation, our evaluation systems indicated that we had reached a brief plateau in overall performance. To break free from this leveling-off stage, we decided to provide more assistance for Business Teams that needed help, and more freedom and positive reinforcement for the more advanced teams. Both actions, which were discussed with those involved, reflected a timely and appropriate response to a given condition.

The situation required a modification of several systems already in place as well as implementation of changes planned to follow initial implementation;

> . . . Team Coordinators were given additional training.

> . . . During vacation periods, the more advanced teams operated without a Team Coordinator.

> . . . We increased team interaction with vendors to improve parts and processes.

> . . . We implemented team interaction with customers to improve product quality.

> . . . We encouraged team participation in product evaluation programs.

Although that performance plateau was successfully passed as a result of these modifications, we took the further step of planning ahead to the next plateau—a stage we expected to reach about one year later.

We began developing alternatives in order to more fully integrate the support groups (such as process and industrial engineers) into the business teams, and to enlarge our team training program. What remained was of course the most crucial element of timing: the innovative steps would have to be implemented just before the next performance plateau — decidedly a call for **alert** leadership.

The indicators also provided a constant reminder and reinforcement for teams as they improved performance. The indicators demonstrated to the team that progress was being made—an element of unquestioned value in maintaining spirit and motivation as transformation took place.

Recognizing the human need for recognition and acknowledgement, we highlighted the many milestones reached both by individual workers and teams, rewarding these contributors in some way for showing us all a better way to go about our business.

In summary, the implementation process is designed so the entire organization undergoes the development experienced by the Planning Team. To the extent practical, each business team and support team received the same experiences, training and assistance as did the pioneering "critical mass."

Through these experiences each team develops at its own pace the relationships and skills necessary to function effectively. This is accomplished in an organization designed to eliminate barriers and to consistently support team work, employee development, rational analysis and alignment to a common purpose. As each team develops its own supporting philosophy or mission, alignment grows and the ongoing process of improvement gathers momentum.

When this ongoing improvement process is accepted as a legitimate and institutionalized part of the entire organization, that is, as an organic element of the way the business is run on a daily basis, transformation of the workplace has truly begun.

Chapter 16

Training and Team Development

Lest we forget old acquaintances, the progress of Chapter 9's Abbott Bicycle Corporation is well worth looking into. Abbott himself was a changed man. No more chest pains, a good deal less tension and (even his stiffest competitors noticed it) something almost approaching a sunny disposition! Relations with Local 1234 could not have been better—a change that would have been sheer fantasy a few months back. Not that ABC was running in the black—**yet**, or that the company was completely out of the woods. But Mr. Abbott, Jack and the other staff people, and Charlie down at Local headquarters sensed that their survival now and upswing later was more than a pie-in-the-sky, optimistic dream. They had been working hard to make it happen.

The ABC Planning Team had put together a top-notch operating plan. The visits to other plants had paid off handsomely, giving the team real insights into what worked and what did not, and into the ingredients that ABC would have to implement if the company were to be a contender in the competitive bicycle business.

The team recognized the unbeatable value of small-group functioning, of democratic participation, of open communication in all directions and of a genuinely thorough network approach to business operations. This total concept was behind every item in the ABC Operating Plan: its overhauled structure, its new systems and oper-

153

ations, a fresh approach to pay and job classifications, a radically changed work environment—everything that reflected life on the plant floor and the relationships within the entire organization.

Incorporating minor changes and a few suggestions for improvement, the combined ABC management and Local leadership accepted the operating plan. It was the right move for everyone concerned. (Besides, Abbott was secretly delighted to get rid of that awful tie and come to work in comfortable clothes!)

The orientation sessions with the workforce were more successful than anyone could have hoped for. But it was far from being an easy-going romp: The workers questioned **everything**; they were skeptical and anxious; some were openly fearful that the Business Team concept might wipe out the whole foundation of their work lives.

Abbott, Jack, Charlie, the Planning Team and all the others present understood these deep concerns and were fully prepared to address them directly and honestly. They spoke openly about ABC's past errors and hopes for the future, about the threat of competition, about business trends and the inadequacy of traditional organization structures and practices in the face of those trends. They looked closely at the existing company and compared its systems and structures with the changes proposed in the new operating plan. For those workers who chose to hear more and taste a sample of this new approach, the leadership provided a session of team-development exercises and another in problem-solving and decision-making training. They reviewed the plan in detail and answered more questions.

When the orientation ended, the option to get involved or not was up to each and every worker—a free choice based on full disclosure. The response was overwhelmingly positive, although a small percentage of the workforce declined the invitation to throw in their lot in the future of the new Abbott Bicycle Corporation. Abbott and the others would have it no other way: participation had to be voluntary. Those who chose not to join were invited to work in the repair department— which would remain as it had always been. Those who chose to join had become the core of ABC's team effort and the heart of its transformation.

At this point in its evolution from the "old" to the "new," Mr. Abbott's company—like all other organizations similarly concerned with a return to a sound footing through restructuring—confronted the need for **appropriate** management at all levels. To function effectively in an environment where participative problem solving and decision making is encouraged, it is clear that management and supervisory personnel **must** have a predisposition to democratic team practices, to the concept of full and active participation. These same people must also have the skills or training required in such an environment or, lacking these, the capacity and willingness to acquire them.

Abbott's company did not have the total flexibility to select an appropriate staff. (Conditions, as we know, vary from place to place.) Four key supervisors were selected using a three-step assessment process designed by the Planning Team. The assessment center helped assure that appropriate choices were made. Those current supervisors deemed to be least suited to the new organization would be in charge of the repair department. (When Charlie watched hourly employees and representatives from Local 1234 trained as assessors, with a real voice in selecting supervisors, he said to himself, "I never thought I'd see the day. This time it's for real!")

From now on ABC Corporation, using the new selection process on an ongoing basis, would in time create a whole management team possessing new attitudes and new skills.

The factors contributing to ABC's turnaround were also vital to the change process at the Livonia engine plant.

Training and Development

Once selected, an hourly and salaried workforce is ready for training and team building. An organization's available time, budget and inherent pool of skills will dictate the kinds and number of training techniques it will adopt to prepare its personnel to function in the new work environment. Whatever those techniques may be, however, they will include, in some form or other, at least two phases: a continuation of the enlightenment process begun during orientation and a skill-development phase that works toward team development. At Livonia we profited by the inclusion of offsite training **before** the participants began day-to-day involvement on the plant floor.

Development of the Operating Staff

Their existing predisposition to a participative style of management greatly simplified the enlightenment process for Livonia's operating staff. As a result their training more quickly focused on experiential team building and on familiarization with the plant, its operations and its systems.

These objectives were met in an offsite workshop session that lasted several days, encompassing the following issues:

- an expanded discussion of competition and its impact on quality and productivity, both domestically and in the world market

- an extensive review of Livonia's product, processes and equipment, including technical training in computer applications and statistical process control

- a review of basic behavioral science principles as applied to the development of the Business Team approach at Livonia

- advanced training in problem solving, decision making, potential problem analysis and performance problem solving

- training in the art of situational management

- refinement of key performance indicators, both for the operating staff and the rest of the plant personnel

Once this preparatory work was done, the Livonia staff was ready to work together to help translate the plan into reality on the plant floor. Working in small groups and continuing the use of rational processes, the staff accomplished this transition by addressing such major implementation concerns as:

What are the most effective ways to help develop our Team Coordinators' skills and comfort in dealing with their new responsibilities?

What are the best and most effective methods for handling technical problems during start-up?

How can we most effectively implement our communication and performance feedback systems?

Dealing with these and other real-life problems gave the operating team the opportunity to ease into its new roles and responsibilities—a sort of slow walk into the cold waters before it was time to dive in altogether! (The presence of members of the Livonia Planning Team on the staff greatly sped up the process; without them, the staff would have required proportionally more training and involvement in the team-building process.)

Once thrown into the demands of daily plant life, the staff profited by continuing the group momentum built up during its training phases. This positive direction was assured by regularly scheduled meetings to review progress and deal with implementation concerns as they came up.

First-Level Supervisor

Training and team building for Team Coordinators consisted of three separate steps:

Phase One: Understanding and Enlightenment

This work for Livonia supervisors was carried out during an offsite workshop period, similar to the process for the operating staff—definitely a preferred context for the important initial phase.

We found it valuable too—as other organizations will—to include operating staff members in these sessions in the spirit of active and full participation.

This phase is devoted extensively to a clear presentation of the expectations placed on all Team Coordinators: their role in the Business Team environment, their responsibilities and the part they must play within the total organization.

Phase Two: The Use of Rational Techniques

Training at this stage concentrates on the development of skill and comfort in using rational approaches to problem solving and decision making.

Team Coordinators already identified as potential teachers of these techniques (done during the selection process) are given an extra week of training, preparing them to lead their own training classes for the hourly workforce. Other supervisors are taught to assist these future trainers. All Team Coordinators, however, begin together in a basic one-week course in these rational approaches.

Phase Three: Application and Cross-Discipline Training

This phase is devoted, in part, to the application of problem-solving and decision-making techniques to specific, real-life implementation concerns. (One solution, for example, dealt with the participants' own assignments to various shifts and departments.)

The cross-discipline training led Team Coordinators to instruct each other in the basics of their particular specializations—production technology, quality control techniques and so on.

The Hourly Workforce

Quality Operator training and team building were initiated in a one-week workshop, with each Business Team intact, wherever possible. The trainers were the Team Coordinators, thus giving these supervisors additional experience and furthering the team-building process.

Phase 1: The Use of Rational Techniques

This step focused on problem solving and decision making, using specific situations drawn from the experiences of real-world organizations.

Phase 2: Team Building

These sessions consisted of group exercises that emphasized the need for trust, communication and problem solving by the group acting in concert.

To "break the ice" for each Business Team, and give its members an opportunity to get to know one another, the group also participated in a simplified version of the "Johari Window" exercise.

Phase 3: Application of the Decision Making Process

To get its first taste of this process in action, each Business Team was asked to develop candidate qualifications for an Assistant Team Coordinator, a role to be filled from the team's own ranks. The exercise in decision making was facilitated by each team's Coordinator.

Phase 4: Understanding the Product

At this stage each Quality Operator disassembled and reassembled a complete engine—plainly the most direct way to get to know one's product!

The team then had the opportunity to direct specific questions to a panel of operating staff members, vendor representatives, product engineers, process engineers and union officials.

Multiple levels of training—for the operating and supervisory staff and for the hourly workforce—are the necessary beginnings of individual groups and development of business team members.

Keeping things in perspective, however, makes clear that these phases of training and team building are beginnings only; successful growth must come in day-to-day confrontations with every aspect of industrial life in a real plant staffed by real people. Consistency is the key to this evolutionary process: consistent with effort, consistent application methods, and, above all, consistent support from an organization designed to remove barriers and encourage individual and team growth as part of its underlying philosophy.

REVIEW/GUIDELINES/APPLICATION

Using Training on Product and Performance Concerns

The Livonia Planning Team used situation appraisal, problem analysis and decision analysis to help develop an overall operating plan and to arrive at workable alternatives to be included in that plan. These same techniques would now be used by individual Business Teams to solve problems and make decisions on a day-to-day basis.

As the result of rational analysis and business team meetings, several more efficient methods have been uncovered, several potentially serious quality problems have been avoided and the plant has had numerous $10,000 team suggestion awards — the highest award allowable under the program.

Almost all Business Teams now understand how statistical process control, the forty key indicators and rational problem solving and decision making lead to continuous improvement in all areas. The connection between rational analysis and improvements in quality, productivity and quality of worklife was difficult for teams to understand during the initial training sessions.

Two real world examples described by the Kepner-Tregoe organization helped Business Teams understand this connection. Even though the examples came from a utility and not from the auto industry, they helped the teams understand early on the value of training in problem solving and decision making.

The first example involves a maintenance employee who had the job of changing a light bulb on smoke-stacks several hundred feet in the air. The light bulbs were part of a sensing unit that was used to determine the amount of opaque particulate matter in the smoke rising in the stack. Changing these light bulbs was the most distasteful part of this maintenance man's job. For years he had to climb the stacks several times a week in the cold of winter and the heat of summer to change burned-out light bulbs.

Using problem analysis, the maintenance employee first described the problem in terms of what it was, where it was, when it occurred and to what extent it occurred. Arraying the information for the first time, it became evident that over 70% of the time he had to change a light bulb that was in stack number one and not in stack number two or three.

Once a problem is described, the problem analysis methodology then teaches employees to look for distinctions, comparing where the problem is, and where the problem is not. In searching for distinctions the maintenance man found a small transformer missing in stack number one. This transformer stepped down the electrical current to be compatible with the light bulbs being used in the smoke-stacks.

As a result of this solution, the maintenance man reduced by 60% the number of times he had to engage in the most distasteful part of his job, climbing the stacks to replace light bulbs. The saving to the company was not great. However, this example demonstrates how solving the small day-to-day operating problems not only improves quality and productivity, but quality of worklife by eliminating nagging problems.

The second example involved a machine repairman called to repair a large generator which had been shut-down. There were three large generators at this plant and when one generator was shut-down, 33 1/3% of capacity was lost. In dismantling the turbine, the machine repairman found a ball bearing had destroyed the fins inside the mechanism. Unfortunately, the turbine would have to be repaired and would be out of service for weeks.

The machine repairman discovered that a small check-valve mechanism adjacent to the turbine contained a ball bearing assembly. The ball bearing assembly had disintegrated and three ball bearings were missing. In addition to the one ball bearing found in the turbine, two more were found inching toward the turbine in a pipe which flowed into the turbine area.

The machine repairman replaced the check-valve with a new mechanism. Had it not been for recently completing a problem analysis course, this would have been the end of the story. However, the last step in problem analysis teaches problem solvers to ask one question, "Where else will this solution likely solve a problem?"

The machine repairman dismantled the check-valves leading to the other two turbines. Upon dismantling the valves, the ball bearings fell apart in his hands. Indeed in one of the pipes leading to the second turbine, a ball bearing was already inching its way to the turbine area. As a result of using problem analysis, this machine repairman saved weeks of down time and literally saved the company close to a million dollars.

This example shows how productivity can be greatly enhanced, not by working harder but by working smarter.

Using problem analysis and decision analysis, the Business Teams at Livonia have chalked up numerous examples similar to those cited above. This is true not only because the training provided the skills, but weekly team meetings provided the opportunity for continued use.

Business Teams proved to themselves through key indicators, that eliminating agonizing problems on the job improved quality, productivity and quality of worklife.

Trained Business Teams are the building block upon which transformation is built. As problems are solved and performance improves, a sense of pride emerges as the human potential inside an organization is realized.

Chapter 17

Personal Rewards and Organizational Results

When we put resources to work for us, it is reasonable to expect a return on that investment. This is as true of human resources as it is of capital. In workplace transformation, while there is of course a capital investment involved, the focus is nonetheless on human concerns: the shift from adversarial relationships to cooperation and mutual support, a new evaluation of the individual as a freely participating contributor, a new respect for the organization as an intimate community of equal partners in a shared goal.

In any enterprise that focuses on human resources, there is a nontraditional time scheme that must be appreciated. Where a machine has a clearly understood lifespan, or an oil well a reasonably predictable depletion rate, no such convenient timetable exists to accurately forecast human growth, development and maturity. Transformation, therefore, is not a quick investment with only short-term results. It is a process that depends on the individual human being and on his or her adaptability to new behaviors; it is a dynamic process that depends on the coming together of these individuals, working in ensemble and growing together in harmony.

What happened, and is happening, at Livonia is only one story among many possible scenarios. It reflects who we are, the degree of our motivation, our business history, the physical state of our plant and so on. Under different conditions the rate of our growth and the

163

degree of our achievements would certainly have been different. Without a state-of-the-art plant it would have taken longer to reach certain goals. Without strong leadership support the evolutionary process would have been more visibly drawn out. That we made significant strides after only one year of operation reflects these conditions.

Other organizations, existing under their own unique conditions, will have their own scenarios and timetables. But whatever those results may be, and however long they will take to occur, a state of improvement can only begin with a marked change in attitudes and perceptions that affect behavior, performance and commitment—in essence, in changes in that organization's "culture." Those changes, moreover, must be part of an integrated and comprehensive process of **total** change. Fragmentation and piecemeal approaches, as we have said so often, are no answer at all; they can amount to little more than momentarily attractive, but eventually futile, stop-gap measures. Industrial good health—given the unrelenting demands of current competition and indeed of pure survival—depends on the wholehearted implementation of a solid overall operating plan wholly consistent with a fundamental business philosophy—all based on a new appreciation of **human** values. We know of no other realistic road to take.

A small sampling of the accomplishments at Livonia demonstrate that quality, productivity and quality of worklife can improve continuously together.

> **Quality**: When measured against conformity to specification (by monthly General Motors audits), consistency of quality reached to within a point or two of perfection.

> Warranty demands were significantly reduced in frequency and cost as compared to previous engines.

> Dealer and customer satisfaction rose perceptibly, eliciting high praise and evidence of acceptance and satisfaction, often in a 95% bracket.

> **Schedule**: While the plant was originally scheduled to operate at approximately 600 engines per day, increased demand moved this figure to 900 in the first year and to 1100 at the start of the second year. Although some overtime was required to meet these unexpected increases, all targets were met.

> **Cost**: The trend line for actual cost-per-engine has significantly declined, and continues to do so. In the first year the

reduction was 50%. Many factors such as scrap, quality, injuries, grievances and inventory contribute to cost reduction. (For our analyses of percentage increases in positive factors and of percentage decreases in negative factors, see Chapter 12.)

Employee Suggestions: Livonia represented approximately 45% of **all** suggestions received throughout the total organization—a total, in the first year, of **ten times** the rate per employee in other plants.

As a result of these suggestions, cost savings at Livonia were approximately $1,400,000 with 700 suggestions still under investigation as of this writing. Team suggestions generated nearly twice the savings per suggestion as individual suggestions.

Pride: Over the course of the first year of operations, management has received numerous and still increasing requests by employees to bring their families into the plant, on their own time, to show them where and how they work and to visit the complete facilities.

Attitude: Quality of worklife surveys were administered at the beginning and end of the first year of operation. These results demonstrated significant gains in both mean and overall percentage responses. Consistent "plus" values concerned (a) on-the-job development and use, (b) employee involvement and influence, (c) relations with supervisor, (d) work-group relations, (e) respect for the individual, (f) confidence in management's understanding, (g) union-management relations and (h) overall quality of worklife.

Without exception the response from visitors to Livonia has reflected an overall impression consistent with our goals: of cooperation, teamwork, commitment, progress and dedication of the entire workforce and staff to the highest quality and productivity levels obtainable. This interest in what we have done has gone far beyond the boundaries of General Motors itself. We have welcomed observers from Ford, Chrysler, Volkswagen, Nissan, Xerox and IBM, and industry executives from Germany, Sweden, Austria, Belgium, Japan and Australia. Other visitors have included William J. Abernathy and Kim E. Clark of the Harvard Graduate School of Business; G. L. Wilson, MIT's Dean of Engineering, and Harry C. Katz, from the Sloan School of Management; James S. Coleman, professor of sociology at the University of Chicago and a former member of a presidential Science Advisory Committee; and representatives of *The Wall Street Journal, National Geographic, ABC-TV* and numerous other trade and media organizations.

We include a sampling of their comments to reflect our pride in the positive results from our hard work to attain our organizational goals:

". . . when you get the best people in the world working together like they are in this plant . . . there isn't any limit to what can be done.

"The plant management, the union and the employees working together have established a relationship based on mutual respect, co-operation and trust that should be the model — and envy — of every plant in the U.S. — inside and outside GM."

Roger B. Smith
Chairman of the Board
General Motors Corporation

When asked about the maximum capacity of the plant, Edward C. Kennard, General Manager, Cadillac; V.P., GMC, responded, "This group can do just about anything they make up their minds to do: they proved it last year."

Alfred S. Warren, GM Vice-President in charge of personnel and industrial relations said: "Among quality of work-life and productivity improvement efforts, the Livonia Plant is a star."

"This plant is outstanding among GM plants in that all people are busy; there are no people standing around, casually talking, reading magazines or just waiting on something."

Farno I. Green
Executive Engineer
Manufacturing Development
General Motors Corpora-
tion

"Your business team approach to management of all elements of the business is impressive. It was obvious that you have done a remarkable job of implementing a complex program involving considerable change in the operating styles and attitudes of many employees.''

John A. Manoogian
Executive Director
Product Assurance
Ford, North American Automotive
Operations

"I am extremely impressed by the novel programs underway within your plant.''

Harry C. Katz
Associate Professor of
Economics and Management
Massachusetts Institute of
Technology
Alfred P. Sloan School of
Management

"It is clear to me that you have an exciting program underway which, in many respects, is unique among the major metalcutting facilities I have visited during the past several years. You have come a long way in a very short period of time.''

George R. Tappert
General Manager
Carboloy Systems Department
General Electric Company

"If only other plants in this country were planned and operated with such common sense and technical skill it would seem we shouldn't have to waste so much time wondering why we've not been able to compete satisfactorily in the international market.''

Treadwell L. Ireland, M.D.,
(Visitor from Florida)

"Your bulletin boards, located in strategic areas of the plant, show recognition of the employee's ability to effectively use information . . . one felt a total effort toward your goal of manufacturing high quality engines."

Peter G. Fotiu, Ed.D.
Licensed Psychologist
(Visitor from Livonia,
Michigan)

"This is the best story I've covered at GM in years."

Hugh Wells
Former News Reporter
Currently Editor, GM Today

"This plant is fantastic," Mark Meed, W.T.V.S., Channel 56. Mr. Meed interviewed five employees and was impressed with their commitment and attitude. He asked one employee, "What makes you think this 4.1 litre engine is any better than one built by Buick or even Mercedes?" The employee responded, "I put my heart in this engine." Mr. Meed stated this was typical of the responses he received from other employees.

"I've never been in a plant like this before with such a friendly atmosphere."

John McElroy
Chilton's Automotive Industry

"Observers say that although Ford has put employee participation programs in more of its plants than GM, the Buick and Cadillac projects are considered to be the most advanced."

Business Week
June 14, 1982

The Livonia experiment was ambitious but it was not without mistakes made along the way. The initial improvements made at Livonia are now an integral part of the plant's day-to-day operations.

Livonia is a vital and vibrant environment and has withstood a change in plant management, the addition of a second shift, growth in employment from 400 to 1400 and an ever increasing production schedule. Despite its imperfections, we have extracted a blueprint for workforce transformation which has been successfully adapted to other plants in other industries.

This is the end of the beginning of the Livonia story, for the philosophy that supports us is also a philosophy that has at its center a permanently open door toward greater maturity and higher levels of evolution. That this invitation into a stronger, more realistic and more humane future need not be limited to American industry alone is clear to us. It remains only for the network of human beings—**without industrial, state or national boundaries**— to risk an exploration of its own vast promise.

The Union Perspective

Irving Bluestone, retired United Auto Workers (U.A.W.) Vice President and Director of the union's General Motors (G.M.) Department, was the international union official who initially approved and endorsed the Livonia Plant Project. Mr. Bluestone is currently University Professor of Labor Studies at Wayne State University. His comments provide a unique insight into the views of a progressive and influential union leader concerning improvement approaches such as the Business Team approach.

Mr. Bluestone initially proposed to GM the adoption of the quality of worklife (QWL) concept, with emphasis on employee involvement in decision making. This proposal culminated in the letter of understanding between the UAW and GM, dated November 19, 1973, establishing the UAW-GM National Committee to Improve the Quality of Work Life.

In my thirty-eight years with the UAW, I participated in countless hard core bargaining sessions with General Motors Corporation at both the national level and the local plant level. The collective bargaining relationship in the US is characterized by an adversarial climate, strong debate over highly controversial issues, and occasional crises. In the years ahead the adversarial aspects of labor-management relationships will no doubt continue to play a significant role in advancing the standard of living of workers and their families and in improving the working conditions.

It is equally true, however, that a vast array of subjects related to managing the workplace and managing the enterprise are, indeed, not adversarial in nature, but are subject to joint problem-solving efforts as matters of common and mutual concern. As to these issues the negotiating parties have a stake in undertaking, jointly, initiatives which are designed to achieve mutually desirable objectives.

Solving problems at the workplace should not lie solely in the domain of managerial prerogatives. In fact, in its practical application, problem solving must be rooted in a process which affords workers the opportunity for meaningful participation in the decision-making process. In this sense, "improving the quality of worklife" represents a further step toward fulfillment of a persistent, historic objective of unionism: to bring, to the extent feasible, democratic values and procedures into the workplace.

Such an approach to the use of human resources in business organizations marks a sharp break with traditional and accepted orthodox work structure and work organization. It is proving its value in hundreds of organizations throughout the country, enhancing the employees' sense of dignity and self-fulfillment, increasing job satisfaction, improving overall efficiency, productivity and quality of product or service and meeting the competitive challenge of the marketplace.

The approach at the Cadillac engine plant in Livonia represents a new development, which characterizes the Livonia plant as a unique and exciting adventure in new directions for union and management relations.

Union and Hourly Employee Involvement From The Inception of An Improvement Effort

Truly successful endeavors in participatory decision making are not developed by management and simply handed down to the union and the workforce. A successful QWL improvement program derives from mutually agreed upon understandings in which the union and management are co-equal in planning, designing and implementing the employee involvement process. The Business Team approach implemented at Cadillac's Livonia engine plant was born and has been maturing as just such a joint effort.

The Heart of Any Improvement Effort Must Be The Upgrading of The Role, Contribution, and Quality of Worklife of the Entire Workforce.

It has often been said that "human dignity is what it's all about." The overall objective must be to upgrade the development, training, participation and quality of working life of the employees at all levels. Sustained development of a workplace climate aimed toward enhancing one's sense of self-worth and self-fulfillment will result in overall improved quality and service and improved efficiency.

As demonstrated by the operating philosophy at Livonia, the Business Team approach was built upon a set of principles which give full recognition to the overriding importance of human dignity. The union officials and hourly workforce participated in designing and implementing the overall approach. They participate, moreover, in assessment teams which select the plant supervision. This is a first in General Motors, and, I believe, in the entire automotive industry.

The extensive training, development, and ongoing participation and cooperation fulfill the basic principles underlying the Business Team approach and hold promise for the continued growth and success of the Livonia plant.

The Collective Bargaining Role Must Not Be Usurped By An Improvement Effort.

Unions have and will always have the legal and moral responsibility to protect fairly and aggressively the rights of their members. There will be a continuing need to use a grievance procedure and engage in collective bargaining negotiations. The representation collective bargaining role of the union cannot be jeopardized.

This is not to say that collective bargaining agreements cannot be altered to meet mutually desirable objectives of the QWL process, subject of course to the bargaining process and membership ratification. At Livonia, for example, the traditional wage and classification structure was altered to accommodate the pay-for-knowledge wage system. I expect the natural progression will lead to gain-sharing programs, in which the workers receive financial or other benefits as their fair share in the improved performance of the enterprise.

The fact that grievances at Livonia are one-tenth of what would be generated under a traditional system, that absenteeism is one-half the normal rate and that demands at contract time will more than likely be expeditiously and equitably resolved is not evidence of erosion of the union's role. It is, rather, proof that the union at Livonia is performing its expanded role every day, satisfying the needs of its members, instead of reacting only when problems arise.

The Final Essential Characteristic Is That Improvement in Effectiveness Cannot Lead to Layoffs in the Workforce.

Corporations and unions must be innovative enough to use the capacity generated by increased effectiveness. The improved ability to compete effectively should lead to more stable employment and enhanced job security. In fact, the increased quality and efficiency at Livonia have upgraded demand and over 400 employees have been added to the workforce.

Continued growth and increasing prosperity are dependent on becoming and remaining viably competitive in the global economy. During the process of becoming competitive, an overriding consideration, as far as the workers are concerned, is that the QWL improvement process must not result in layoffs, in a threat to employment security. This is established as a fundamental guideline in the design of the process.

The Business Team approach meets the basic requirements for an appropriate union-management effort. It represents a significant step toward continued growth and security for the enterprise and its workforce—an outgrowth of the "Quality of Worklife Improvement" concept that was incorporated into the National Agreement between GM and the UAW in 1973.

The principles outlined above set forth sound requirements for an appropriate joint QWL improvement effort. In practical application, union and management operate as co-equal actors in advancing the role of the worker in the process, as follows:

- Greater autonomy for the workforce.

- Increased participation in decision making.

- Improved employee training.

- Quality improvement.

- Innovative compensation approaches.

- Reduced absenteeism.

- Reduced labor turnover.

- Employee health and personal development.

- Improvement in competitive position.

A process such as the one at Livonia requires initially the development of a climate of mutual respect and trust between the union and the employees on the one hand and the management team on the other. It calls for open, candid two-way communication and a deep appreciation by management of the innate capabilities, the creativity, and the innovative capacities of all the employees.

It takes considerable courage and foresight for the representatives of management and of the union to break with tradition and move toward exciting and challenging new directions of work structure and work organization. The UAW and GM at the Cadillac engine plant in Livonia have embarked on such a course, devoted to the principles of co-equality, of involvement, of cooperative effort. This certainly bodes well for a bright future of joint accomplishment.

Irving Bluestone

About The Authors

The authors collectively possess sixty-five years of expertise in business and industry. Their varied experiences and educational backgrounds were synergistically brought together in a unique endeavor to improve product quality, quality of worklife and productivity at a technologically advanced engine plant in Livonia, Michigan, operated by Cadillac Motor Car Division, General Motors Corporation.

JOHN J. NORA

Jack's industrial experience began as an hourly employee on Cadillac Motor Cars' final assembly line. He progressed through various assignments including hourly employee; production foreman; organizational development coordinator; manager of human resource development; and divisional head of quality of worklife for Cadillac Motor Car Company.

Jack's educational background includes a Bachelor of Arts from Michigan State University, majoring in personnel management; an MBA from the University of Detroit, majoring in organization and human behavior; and Juris Doctors Degree, summa cum laude, from the University of Detroit School of Law.

His involvement at Livonia was as the initial strategist, Planning Team facilitator, and personnel administrator. After leaving General Motors, Jack became an attorney associated with Dickinson, Wright,

Moon, Van Dusen & Freeman, a large defense law firm in Detroit, where he specialized in labor and employment law.

Currently, Jack consults with select clients and Kepner-Tregoe, a Princeton-based consulting firm, concerning the transformation process. Jack is also a shareholder in the law firm, Nora, Hemming, Law, Essad and Polaczyk, P.C., in Plymouth, Michigan. He also works with Kepner-Tregoe's Human Performance Group consulting with select clients concerning the transformation process.

C. RAYMOND ROGERS

Ray's industrial experience includes Bell Telephone Corporation, exchange manager; Dale Carnegie, Inc., associate sponsor; Trane Company, director of human resource development and general manager of the Chicago Residential Center; Heil-Quaker Corporation, director of human resource development and general manager of marketing and sales. Ray is currently managing director of Kepner-Tregoe's Human Performance Group.

Ray received degrees from Lincoln College and Grinnell College, where he graduated with honors.

His involvement at Livonia was as the outside consultant for the project. He consulted with the organization concerning the overall improvement strategy. He also designed and implemented several creative approaches to team development and training.

ROBERT J. STRAMY

Bob began his career with General Motors and Cadillac Motor Car Division as a junior engineer. He progressed through the positions of senior paint engineer, senior engineer in advanced processes; assistant superintendant in advanced processes and forward planning; assistant master mechanic; director of process engineering; general superintendent in engine component machining and assembly; and plant manager, Livonia engine plant.

Bob's educational background includes a Bachelor of Science from General Motors Institute, majoring in industrial engineering, and a Sloan Fellowship to the Graduate School of Business, Stanford University.

His initial involvement at the Livonia plant was in strategy development and as a member of the Planning Team. As plant manager, Bob had the responsibility for successful implementation from 1981 until June of 1984, when he was promoted and became manager of General Motors engine facilities in Saltillo, Mexico. Bob is now confirming the international application of the transformation process.

Footnotes

1 Owen Bieber, *Chilton's Iron Age*, Vol. 226, May 11, 1983.

2 Robert B. Reich, "The Next American Frontier," *Atlantic Monthly*, March 1983, page 48.

3 *Ibid.*

4 *Business Week* (Special Issue), June 30, 1980.

5 William J. Abernathy, Kim B. Clark, Alan M. Kantrow, *Industrial Renaissance*, New York: Basic Books, 1983, page 85. Reprinted by permission of the publisher. (A quotation from *Industrial Renaissance* also appears on the cover of this book.)

6 *Ibid.*, pages 90 and 92.

7 Irving Bluestone, *Chilton's Iron Age*, Vol. 225, March 10, 1982.

8 Edward Lawler is Director of The Center for Organizational Effectiveness at the University of Southern California Graduate School of Business. His findings appear in the article "Human Resource Productivity in the 80's," *New Management*, Spring 1983, pages 46-50.

9 *Chilton's Iron Age*, Vol. 225, March 10, 1982.

10 Among the resources available for such exercises we recommend *A Handbook of Structured Experiences for Human Relations Training*, Volumes 1 - 5, William J. Pfeiffer and John E. Jones, Iowa City, Iowa: University Associates Press, 1969.

11 Training at Livonia in rational approaches to problem solving and decision making—which began with the Planning Team and eventually included the entire workforce—was undertaken in cooperation with Kepner-Tregoe, Inc., Princeton, New Jersey, a multinational corporation engaged in organization development and research.

The material presented in this section, including the designations "Situation Appraisal," "Problem Analysis," "Potential Problem Analysis" and "Decision Analysis," while offered without quotation marks or further attribution, has been developed from our Kepner-Tregoe consulting work and is available in *The New Rational Manager*, Charles H. Kepner and Benjamin B. Tregoe (Princeton, N.J.: Princeton Research Press, 1981), a publication that explains the principles of this training. By permission.

12   This description and illustration of the Johari Window are taken verbatim by permission from Ronald J. Fisher, *Social Psychology: An Applied Approach*, New York: St. Martin's Press, 1982, pages 214-215.

13   William Ouchi, *Theory Z*, New York: Addison-Wesley, 1981, page 131.

14   If there **is** an Abbott Bicycle Corporation, our apologies for reinventing its name. Any connection between our ABC and theirs is strictly coincidental and unintentional.

15   Robert B. Reich, ''The Next American Frontier.''

16   Rensis Likert, *New Patterns of Management*, New York: McGraw-Hill, 1961, page 104.

17   Ronald J. Fisher, *Social Psychology: An Applied Approach*, page 368.

18   Ibid, pages 360-361.

19   ''Concessionary Bargaining: Will the New Cooperation Last?'' *Business Week*, June 14, 1982.